The Syrian Goddess

(De Dea Syria)

Society of Biblical Literature
Text and Translations
Graeco-Roman Religion Series

Edited by
Edward N. O'Neil
and
Hans Dieter Betz

TEXTS AND TRANSLATIONS 9

GRAECO-ROMAN RELIGION SERIES 1

THE SYRIAN GODDESS

(DE DEA SYRIA)

by

HAROLD W. ATTRIDGE

AND

ROBERT A. ODEN

SCHOLARS PRESS

The Syrian Goddess

(De Dea Syria)

Attributed to Lucian

by

Harold W. Attridge

and

Robert A. Oden

Published by

SCHOLARS PRESS

FOR

THE SOCIETY OF BIBLICAL LITERATURE

THE SYRIAN GODDESS

(DE DEA SYRIA)

ATTRIBUTED TO LUCIAN

by

Harold W. Attridge

and

Robert A. Oden

Copyright © 1976

by

THE SOCIETY OF BIBLICAL LITERATURE

LIBRARY OF CONGRESS CATALOGING IN PUBLICATION DATA
Lucianus Samosatensis.
 The Syrian goddess=(De dea Syria).

 (Graeco-Roman religion series) (Texts and transla-
tions ; 9)
 1. Hierapolis, Asia Minor — Religion. 2. Cultus —
Hierapolis, Asia Minor. I. Title. II. Series.
III. Series: Society of Biblical Literature. Texts
and translations ; 9.
BL1060.L7813   299'.275'691   76-135
ISBN 0-89130-073-2

PRINTED IN THE UNITED STATES OF AMERICA
2 3 4 5

Printing Department
University of Montana
Missoula, Montana 59801

PREFACE

A preliminary version of this translation was prepared for a class in ancient religious literature at Harvard Divinity School, when it became apparent that no useable translation of the *De Dea Syria* was available. The Loeb edition, with text and translation by A. M. Harmon is an interesting attempt to render some of the flavor of the Ionic dialect of the piece by utilizing an archaizing English. The results, however, leave something to be desired from the point of view of readability. This edition should make this interesting and important document more generally and readily accessible.

The translation has been the primary responsibility of Mr. Attridge; the introduction, of Mr. Oden, although both contributed to the whole project. Prof. Edward N. O'Neil, of the University of Southern California, deserves a special word of appreciation. He made many valuable suggestions on both text and translation and saved the authors from numerous errors and infelicities. Our thanks also to Prof. H. D. Betz for accepting this piece for the Texts and Translations series.

TABLE OF CONTENTS

INTRODUCTION

It is difficult to overstate the case for the importance of *The Syrian Goddess* to the student of ancient religion. After guiding us on à Cook's Tour through various
renowned shrines of Phoenicia, the work's author leads his
readers to Hierapolis (ancient Mabbūg, modern Mambij),
whose myths he recounts and whose temple and cult he de-
scribes in detail. The accounts and descriptions, claims
the author, are based upon information he obtained himself
in visiting the "Holy City" and in questioning the city's
inhabitants, some of whom were well versed in the city's
holy lore. It is in this claim to a firsthand knowledge
of Hierapolis' religious traditions, a claim substantiated
by other accounts ancient and modern,[1] that the unique
value of *The Syrian Goddess* lies. Other roughly contem-
porary descriptions of the religion of Hierapolis, or of
the pagan religion of Phoenicia and Syria in general, are
usually based upon material with a long and complex history of transmission. For example, the Phoenician theol-
ogy attributed to Sakkunyaton, which is valuable despite
the material's problems, as Eissfeldt, Albright, and others have seen,[2] is preserved only in Eusebius' collection
of material from Philo Byblios. The intriguing euhemer-
istic account of various Near Eastern cults, including
that of Mabbūg/Hierapolis, in the *Apology* attributed to
Melito of Sardis, is plainly a distinct and originally
Greek section of this Syriac work.[3] Other descriptions of
the mythic traditions of Phoenicia and Syria in material
from the first four or five centuries of the present era--
one thinks especially of Jacob of Sarug's Syriac homily *On
the Fall of the Idols*, or Moschus' Phoenician theogony as
reported by Damascius[4]--have a similarly complex history
of transmission. *The Syrian Goddess* is both much fuller
and more immediate than any of these; and hence its claim
upon the attention of the student of ancient religion.

1

Authorship

Along with eighty-one other pieces, *The Syrian Goddess* is attributed to the second-century satirist and rhe-
torician Lucian, who was born in Samosata, the capital of
the province of Commagene, but whose literary career carried him throughout the Mediterranean basin. It has become common to stigmatize Lucian as unoriginal if not
plainly second rate; but his *Death of Peregrinus* and *True
Story* are masterful, and the latter was a model for Eras-
mus, Swift, and others. Though the manuscript tradition
is unanimous in ascribing *The Syrian Goddess* to Lucian,
and though the work's Lucianic authorship was long unques-
tioned, the past two centuries have witnessed numerous as-
saults on the work's traditional authorship. Of the cri-
teria used to distinguish *The Syrian Goddess* from the
(certainly genuine) works of Lucian, two stand out: (1)
The Syrian Goddess is composed in Ionic Greek, a dialect
distinct from Lucian's usual Attic and elsewhere parallel-
ed among lengthy works attributed to Lucian only by the
Astrology, which many deny to Lucian;[5] and (2) Lucian's
irrepressible satire is either skillfully hidden in, or
entirely absent from, *The Syrian Goddess*. It is possible
to answer both of these objections, since the pseudo-Ionic
revival of the second century[6] could well have been the
butt of Lucian's satire, perhaps in deliberate parody of
Herodotus, and since there are passages in *The Syrian Goddess* which many have read as typically Lucianic satire.
In the nineteenth century, Jakob Burckhardt defended the
work's authenticity on just these grounds,[7] and Burckhardt's authoritative voice persuaded Theodor Nöldeke,[8]
Franz Cumont,[9] and others; but within the past few years
Hans Dieter Betz, for example, has argued that the sup-
posed hidden satire of *The Syrian Goddess* is hidden indeed, too much so for the work to be considered Lucianic.[10]
The question of authorship is, then, unsettled. Still,
the dialect of *The Syrian Goddess* does suggest a date of
composition in the second century; and the author's

familiarity with the several levels of tradition at Hierapolis may indicate a knowledge of Aramaic and thus perhaps his upbringing in the Near East.

Trustworthiness

The basic trustworthiness of the observations related
in *The Syrian Goddess* is supported by a multitude of evidence and stands independent of the question of authorship.
This is true even if the work is a Lucianic satire, for
effective satire may well have a factual basis, even if
that basis is then exaggerated or fancifully elaborated.
Many of the accounts in *The Syrian Goddess*, even those
which seem most absurd to a modern reader, are confirmed
by parallel descriptions given by Aelian, Macrobius, and
others in antiquity. For example, the bearded, seated
figure in the lesser shrine of the Hierapolis temple is
described similarly in *The Syrian Goddess* and in Macrobius'
Saturnalia (1.17.66-70); and both authors relate that the
city's inhabitants call this deity Apollo. Also, the
presence of sacred fish in the cult of Atargatis, who is
to be identified with the Syrian Goddess, is recounted in
The Syrian Goddess and finds literary confirmation in
Aelian's *On the Nature of Animals* (12.2) and in epigraphic
and archaeological evidence from other Atargatis cult
sites. Visitors to Hierapolis/Mambij in this century have
remarked on the similarity of the sacred area as described
in *The Syrian Goddess* to the traces of this area as visible in modern times.[11] Especially instructive are coins
from Hierapolis. The fourth-century B.C. *'bd-hdd* coinage
portrays the Hierapolis priests with their dress as described in *The Syrian Goddess*.[12] And third-century A.D.
Hierapolis coins of Caracalla and Severus portray the
scene of the inner chamber (*thalamos*) precisely as described in *The Syrian Goddess*.[13] The work's evidence,
then, can be confirmed and is to be relied upon in recon-
structing the religion of Hierapolis.

The Religion of Hierapolis

In keeping with the classical ethnographic tradition, all of the deities of Hierapolis are given Greek names by the author of *The Syrian Goddess*. Thus we read of the divine pair Hera and Zeus, of a bearded Apollo, of Hermes, Atlas, and others. But the author himself admits that the god he labels Zeus is not called Zeus by the natives; and behind each of the other deities named in the work stands a native, Syrian deity. As we know from a host of other testimony, the goddess responsible for the title and named Hera elsewhere in the work is Atargatis. Her name and attributes encompass at least two (`Aštart and `Anat) and probably all three ('Ašerah, `Aštart, and `Anat) major Canaanite goddesses. Her consort Zeus is Ba`l Haddu, one of the lead actors in the Ugaritic myths; and the bearded Apollo is most likely 'Ēl,[14] the grand patriarchal deity of Canaanite religion whose divine decrees are a necessary prelude to the undertaking of any major action. This, at least, is the growing consensus of scholarly opinion, though Strong and Garstang[15] near the beginning of this century and Stocks[16] somewhat later argued for the Anatolian, perhaps originally Hittite, character of the religion of Hierapolis. In any case, despite the Greek names given the deities, the Near Eastern nature of this religion is clear. A steward named Kombabos figures largely in a tale related here; and his name is surely the same as that of Ḫumbaba, the guardian of Ištar's cedar forest in the epic of Gilgameš. The flood legend of *The Syrian Goddess* finds its closest parallels with Semitic deluge myths, especially that of the Hebrew Bible. We have in *The Syrian Goddess* a reliable account in Greek dress of the religion of an important pilgrimage site in the Hellenistic Near East; thus, the work is a source of major significance for the study of the religion of Syria near the beginning of the present era.

Bibliographical Note: Among the lengthier treatments of *The Syrian Goddess*, the most noteworthy are H. Stocks, "Studien zur Lukians 'De Syria Dea,'" *Berytus* 4 (1937)

1-40, and Carl Clemen's *Lukians Schrift über die syrische Göttin* (Der Alte Orient vol. 37 part 3/4; Leipzig: J.C. Hinrichs, 1938), both of which contain full references to earlier studies of the document. There is an excellent bibliography of studies relating both to *The Syrian Goddess* and to Lucian in Hans Dieter Betz, *Lukian von Samosata und das Neue Testament* (Texte und Untersuchungen zur Geschichte der altchristlichen Literatur vol. 76; Berlin: Akademie-Verlag, 1961) 218-251. See also Robert A. Oden, Jr., "Studies in Lucian's *De Syria Dea*" (Harvard 1975), forthcoming in the Harvard Semitic Monograph Series.

NOTES

1. See 3-4 below for references to a number of the
accounts which confirm this claim. An invaluable collection of material relating to the goddess worshipped at
Hierapolis and elsewhere is now available in Paul-Louis
van Berg, *Répertoire des sources grecques et latines: Sauf
le De Dea Syria* (Corpus Cultus Deae Syriae, 1. Les sources
littéraires, première partie; Leiden: E.J. Brill, 1972).

2. See Otto Eissfeldt, *Ras Schamra und Sanchunjaton*
(Beiträge zur Religionsgeschichte des Altertums vol. 4;
Halle: Max Niemeyer, 1939), especially 67-71 and 75-95,
and *Sanchunjaton von Berut und Ilumilku von Ugarit* (Beiträge zur Religionsgeschichte des Altertums vol. 5; Halle:
Max Niemeyer, 1952); and William Foxwell Albright, *Yahweh
and the Gods of Canaan* (Garden City, New York: Doubleday,
1968) 223-226, 244-247, and 259-263, with the references
cited there.

3. The Syriac text of (Pseudo-) Melito's *Apology*,
from a sixth- or seventh-century manuscript now in the
British Museum, together with an English translation, can
be found in William Cureton, *Spicilegium Syriacum* (London:
Rivington, 1855). The case for the Greek origin of this
Apology's section on pagan religion is argued in detail in
the dissertation of Robert A. Oden, Jr. ("Studies in Lucian's *De Syria Dea*," Harvard, 1975).

4. The text of the former was edited by M. l'Abbé
Martin, "Discours de Jacques de Saroug sur la chute des
idoles," *Zeitschrift der deutschen morganländischen Ge-
sellschaft* 29 (1875) 107-147. For Moschus, see, e.g.,
Albright, *Yahweh and the Gods of Canaan* 222-223.

5. A summary statement of the arguments against the
authenticity of the *Astrology* is offered by Hans Dieter
Betz, *Lukian von Samosata und das Neue Testament* (Texte
und Untersuchungen zur Geschichte der altchristlichen Literatur vol. 76; Berlin: Akademie-Verlag, 1961) 25.

6. This revival is reviewed by Francis G. Allinson,
"Pseudo-Ionism in the Second Century A.D.," *American Jour-
nal of Philology* 7 (1886) 203-217.

7. *Die Zeit Constantin's des Grossen* (Leipzig: See-
mann, 1853) 182.

8. "Baethgen's *Beiträge zur semitischen Religionsgeschichte*," ZDMG 42 (1888) 473, n. 4. Nöldeke says spe-
cifically that it was the reasoning of Burckhardt that
persuaded him of the work's authenticity.

9. *Les religions orientales dans le paganisme romain* 4th ed. (Paris: Paul Geuthner, 1929) 12, n. 23.

10. *Lukian von Samosata und das Neue Testament* 24, n. 4. Betz labels the author of *The Syrian Goddess* "der fromme Verfasser" (24).

11. D.G. Hogarth, "Hierapolis Syriae," *Annual of the British School at Athens* 14 (1907-1908) 197; and H. Stocks, "Studien zu Lukians 'De Syria Dea,'" *Berytus* 4 (1937) 1-13.

12. Stocks, "Studien," 5. For a comprehensive study of this coinage, see S. Ronzevalle, "Les monnaies de la dynastie de 'Abd-Hadad et les cultes de Hiérapolis-Bambycé," *Mélanges de l'Université Saint Joseph de Beyrouth* 23 (1940) 1-82.

13. Drawings of these two coins can be seen perhaps most conveniently in Arthur Bernard Cook, *Zeus: A Study in Ancient Religion* vol. 1 (Cambridge: Cambridge University Press, 1914) 586, figs. 448-449, though anyone wishing to see more accurate representations should consult the collections of F. Imhoof-Blumer and Joseph Pellerin, referred to by Cook (586, nn. 4-5). The coins are also pictured or discussed in most modern studies of *The Syrian Goddess*, for which see the Bibliographical Note above.

14. This identification was first suggested by René Dussaud, "Peut-on identifier l'Apollon barbu de Hiérapolis de Syrie?," *Revue de l'histoire des religions* 126 (1943) 147-148, and is now supported by additional evidence about Canaanite 'Ēl.

15. John Garstang and Herbert A. Strong, *The Syrian Goddess* (London: Constable, 1913), especially 11-12.

16. "Studien," 1-40.

The text reprinted here is basically that of the
third edition by K. Jacobitz in the Teubner series (Leipzig, 1910-12). MSS variants and emendations recorded are
those listed in that edition and in the edition of A. M.
Harmon in the Loeb series (London, New York, 1913). Only
variants significant for the translation have been includ-
ed here. For more recent study of the textual tradition
of Lucian, cf. M. Wittek, "Liste des manuscrits de Lucien"
Scriptorium 6 (1952) 309-23, and the new edition in the
Oxford Classical Texts series by M. D. MacLeod (Oxford,
1972), in which the *De Dea Syria* has not yet appeared.

The MSS cited are:
      Γ   Vaticanus 90   saec. X
      E   Harleianus 5694 saec. X
      N   Parisinus 2957   saec. XV

The editions cited are:
      Leh. = Lehmann,   Leipzig, 1822-31
      Dind. = Dindorf,   Leipzig, 1858
      Frit. = Fritzsche, Rostoch, 1860-82
      Jac. = Jacobitz,   Leipzig, 1910-12
      Harm. = Harmon,   London and New York, 1913

      Eds. = Dind. Harm. Jac.

ΠΕΡΙ ΤΗΣ ΣΥΡΙΗΣ ΘΕΟΥ.

1. Ἔστιν ἐν Συρίῃ πόλις οὐ πολλὸν ἀπὸ τοῦ Εὐφρήτεω ποταμοῦ, καλέεται δὲ Ἰρὴ καὶ ἔστιν ἱρὴ τῆς Ἥρης τῆς Ἀσσυρίης. δοκέει δέ μοι, τόδε τὸ οὔνομα οὐκ ἅμα τῇ πόλι οἰκεομένῃ ἐγένετο, ἀλλὰ τὸ μὲν ἀρχαῖον ἄλλο ἦν· μετὰ δὲ σφίσι τῶν ἱρῶν μεγάλων γιγνομένων ἐς τόδε ἡ ἐπωνυμίη ἀπίκετο. περὶ ταύτης ὦν τῆς πόλιος ἔρχομαι ἐρέων ὁκόσα ἐν αὐτῇ ἐστιν· ἐρέω δὲ καὶ νόμους, τοῖσιν ἐς τὰ ἱρὰ χρέονται, καὶ πανηγύριας τὰς ἄγουσι καὶ θυσίας τὰς ἐπιτε- λέουσιν. ἐρέω δὲ ὁκόσα καὶ περὶ τῶν τὸ ἱρὸν εἰσαμένων μυθολογέουσι, καὶ τὸν νηὸν ὅκως ἐγένετο. γράφω δὲ Ἀσσύ- ριος ἐών, καὶ τῶν ἀπηγέομαι τὰ μὲν αὐτοψίῃ ἔμαθον, τὰ δὲ παρὰ τῶν ἱρέων ἐδάην, ὁκόσα ἐόντα ἐμεῦ πρεσβύτερα ἐγὼ ἱστορέω.

2. Πρῶτοι μὲν ὦν ἀνθρώπων, τῶν ἡμεῖς ἴδμεν, Αἰγύπτιοι λέγονται θεῶν τε ἐννοίην λαβεῖν καὶ ἱρὰ εἴσασθαι καὶ τεμένεα καὶ πανηγύριας ἀποδέξαι. πρῶτοι δὲ καὶ οὐνόματα ἱρὰ ἔγνωσαν καὶ λόγους ἱροὺς ἔλεξαν. μετὰ δὲ οὐ πολλοστῷ χρόνῳ παρ' Αἰγυπτίων λόγον Ἀσσύριοι ἐς θεοὺς ἤχουσαν καὶ ἱρὰ καὶ νηοὺς ἤγειραν, ἐν τοῖσι καὶ ἀγάλματα ἔθεντο καὶ ξόανα ἐστήσαντο. 3. τὸ δὲ παλαιὸν καὶ παρ' Αἰγυπτίοισιν ἀξόανοι νηοὶ ἔσαν. καὶ ἔστιν ἱρὰ καὶ ἐν Συρίῃ οὐ παρὰ πολὺ τοῖς Αἰγυπτίοισιν ἰσοχρονέοντα, τῶν ἐγὼ πλεῖστα ὄπωπα· τό γε τοῦ Ἡρακλέος τὸ ἐν Τύρῳ, οὐ τούτου τοῦ Ἡρακλέος, τὸν Ἕλληνες ἀείδουσιν, ἀλλὰ τὸν ἐγὼ λέγω, πολλὸν ἀρχαιότερος, καὶ Τύριος ἥρως ἐστίν.

THE SYRIAN GODDESS

1   In Syria there is a city not far from the Euphrates River. It is called "Hire" (Holy) and it is
the Holy City of the Assyrian Hera.[1] I think that
this was not the name of the city when it was founded,
and the ancient name was different. Later, when their
rites became important, the name was changed to the
present one. Concerning this city I am going to describe whatever is in it. I will tell of the customs
which they observe in connection with the rites, the
festivals which they hold and the sacrifices which
they perform. I will also relate whatever stories
they tell about those who founded the sanctuary and
about how the temple came into being. I write as an
Assyrian, and some of the things I relate I learned
firsthand, but what happened before my time I have
learned from the priests.

2   Now then, the Egyptians are supposedly the first
men who formed a conception of gods, established sanctuaries and sacred precincts and instituted festivals.
They were also the first to conceive of holy names and
to tell sacred tales. Not long afterwards, the Assyrians heard an account about gods from the Egyptians,
and they established sanctuaries and temples in which
3   they placed images and set up statues.--In antiquity,
however, temples among the Egyptians were without a
sanctuary. --In Syria, too, there are sanctuaries al-
most as old as the Egyptian ones. Most of these I
have seen, in particular the one of Heracles at Tyre.
This is not the Heracles whom the Greeks celebrate
in song. The one I mean is much older and is a Tyrian
hero.

---

    1. The word for holy, ἱρή, and the name of the god-
dess would have been pronounced virtually the same.

11

4. ἔνι δὲ καὶ ἄλλο ἰρὸν ἐν Φοινίκῃ μέγα, τὸ Σιδώνιοι
ἔχουσιν, ὡς μὲν αὐτοὶ λέγουσιν, Ἀστάρτης ἐστίν· Ἀστάρτην
δ' ἐγὼ δοκέω Σεληναίην ἔμμεναι· ὡς δέ μοί τις τῶν ἰρέων
ἀπηγέετο, Εὐρώπης ἐστὶ τῆς Κάδμου ἀδελφεῆς. ταύτην δ'
ἐοῦσαν Ἀγήνορος τοῦ βασιλῆος θυγατέρα, ἐπειδή τε ἀφανὴς
ἐγεγόνεεν, οἱ Φοίνικες τῷ νηῷ ἐτιμήσαντο καὶ λόγον ἰρὸν
ἐπ' αὐτῇ ἔλεξαν, ὅτι ἐοῦσαν καλὴν Ζεὺς ἐπόθεε καὶ τὸ εἶδος
εἰς ταῦρον ἀμειψάμενος ἥρπασε, καί μιν ἐς Κρήτην φέρων
ἀπίκετο. τάδε μὲν καὶ τῶν ἄλλων Φοινίκων ἤκουον, καὶ τὸ
νόμισμα, τῷ Σιδώνιοι χρέονται, τὴν Εὐρώπην ἐφεζομένην ἔχει
τῷ ταύρῳ τῷ Διί· τὸν δὲ νηὸν οὐκ ὁμολογέουσιν Εὐρώπης
ἔμμεναι. 5. ἔχουσι δὲ καὶ ἄλλο Φοίνικες ἰρόν, οὐκ Ἀσσύ-
ριον, ἀλλ' Αἰγύπτιον, τὸ ἐξ Ἡλίου πόλιος ἐς τὴν Φοινίκην
ἀπίκετο. ἐγὼ μέν μιν οὐκ ὄπωπα, μέγα δὲ καὶ τόδε καὶ
ἀρχαῖόν ἐστιν. 6. εἶδον δὲ καὶ ἐν Βύβλῳ μέγα ἰρὸν Ἀφροδίτης Βυβλίης, ἐν τῷ καὶ τὰ ὄργια ἐς Ἄδωνιν ἐπιτελέουσιν·
ἐδάην δὲ καὶ τὰ ὄργια. λέγουσι γὰρ δὴ ὧν τὸ ἔργον τὸ ἐς
Ἄδωνιν ὑπὸ τοῦ συὸς ἐν τῇ χώρῃ τῇ σφετέρῃ γενέσθαι καὶ
μνήμην τοῦ πάθεος τύπτονταί τε ἑκάστου ἔτεος καὶ θρηνέουσι
καὶ τὰ ὄργια ἐπιτελέουσιν ,καὶ σφίσι μεγάλα πένθεα ἀνὰ τὴν
χώρην ἵσταται. ἐπεὰν δὲ ἀποτύψωνταί τε καὶ ἀποκλαύσωνται,
πρῶτα μὲν καταγίζουσι τῷ Ἀδώνιδι ὅκως ἐόντι νέκυι, μετὰ
δὲ τῇ ἑτέρῃ ἡμέρῃ ζώειν τέ μιν μυθολογέουσι καὶ ἐς τὸν
ἠέρα πέμπουσι καὶ τὰς κεφαλὰς ξυρέονται ὅκως Αἰγύπτιοι
ἀποθανόντος Ἄπιος. γυναικῶν δὲ ὀκόσαι οὐκ ἐθέλουσι ξυ-
ρέεσθαι, τοιήνδε ζημίην ἐκτελέουσιν·

4   There is another great sanctuary in Phoenicia,
which the Sidonians possess. According to them, it
belongs to Astarte, but I think that Astarte is
Selene. One of the priests, however, told me that it
is a sanctuary of Europa, the sister of Cadmus; that
she was the daughter of Agenor the king, and when she
disappeared, the Phoenicians honored her with a temple
and told a holy tale about her, namely that Zeus desired her since she was beautiful, that he assumed the
form of a bull, seized her, and carried the girl off
with him to Crete. I heard the same tale from the
other Phoenicians as well, and the coinage which the
Sidonians use depicts Europa sitting on the bull,
which is Zeus, but they do not agree that the temple
is that of Europa.

5   The Phoenicians have yet another sanctuary, not
Assyrian but Egyptian, which came[1] to Phoenicia from
Heliopolis. I have not seen it, but it is both large
and ancient.

6   I did see, however, in Byblos a great sanctuary
of Aphrodite of Byblos in which they perform the rites
of Adonis, and I learned about the rites. They say,
at any rate, that what the boar did to Adonis occurred
in their territory. As a memorial of his suffering
each year they beat their breasts, mourn, and celebrate the rites. Throughout the land they perform
solemn lamentations. When they cease their breast-
beating and weeping, they first sacrifice to Adonis
as if to a dead person, but then, on the next day,
they proclaim that he lives and send him into the air.[2]
They also shave their heads, as do the Egyptians when
Apis dies. The women who refuse to shave pay this

1. The verb ἀπικνέομαι occurs in the text frequently
and sometimes with odd meanings.

2. On this ambiguous phrase, cf. R. de Vaux, "Sur
quelques rapports entre Adonis et Osiris" *Revue Biblique*
42 (1933) 43-47. It can refer to a resurrection or an
apotheosis.

14

ἐν μιῇ ἡμέρῃ ἐπὶ πρήσι τῆς ὥρης ἵστανται, ἡ δὲ ἀγορὴ
μούνοισι ξείνοισι παρακέεται καὶ ὁ μισθὸς ἐς τὴν Ἀφροδίτην θυσίη γίγνεται.   7. εἰσὶ δὲ ἔνιοι Βυβλίων, οἳ λέγουσι παρὰ σφίσι τεθάφθαι τὸν Ὄσιριν τὸν Αἰγύπτιον, καὶ
τὰ πένθεα καὶ τὰ ὄργια οὐκ ἐς τὸν Ἄδωνιν, ἀλλ' ἐς τὸν
Ὄσιριν πάντα πρήσσεσθαι.   ἐρέω δὲ ὀκόθεν καὶ τάδε πιστὰ
δοκέουσι.   κεφαλὴ ἑκάστου ἔτεος ἐξ Αἰγύπτου ἐς τὴν Βύβλον
ἀπικνέεται πλώουσα τὸν μεταξὺ πλόον ἑπτὰ ἡμερέων, καί μιν
οἱ ἄνεμοι φορέουσι θείῃ ναυτιλίῃ· τρέπεται δὲ οὐδαμά, ἀλλ'
ἐς μούνην τὴν Βύβλον ἀπικνέεται.   καὶ ἔστι τὸ σύμπαν
θῶυμα.   καὶ τοῦτο[1] ἑκάστου ἔτεος γίγνεται, τὸ καὶ[1] ἐμεῦ
παρεόντος ἐν Βύβλῳ ἐγένετο· καὶ τὴν κεφαλὴν ἐθεησάμην
Βυβλίνην.   8. ἔνι δὲ καὶ ἄλλο θῶυμα ἐν τῇ χώρῃ τῇ Βυβλίνῃ,
ποταμὸς ἐκ τοῦ Λιβάνου τοῦ οὔρεος ἐς τὴν ἅλα ἐκδιδοῖ·
οὔνομα τῷ ποταμῷ Ἄδωνις ἐπικέεται.   ὁ δὲ ποταμὸς ἑκάστου
ἔτεος αἱμάσσεται καὶ τὴν χροιὴν ὀλέσας ἐσπίπτει ἐς τὴν
θάλασσαν καὶ φοινίσσει τὸ πολλὸν τοῦ πελάγεος καὶ σημαίνει
τοῖς Βυβλίοις τὰ πένθεα.   μυθέονται δὲ ὅτι ταύτῃσι τῇσιν
ἡμέρῃσιν ὁ Ἄδωνις ἀνὰ τὸν Λίβανον τιτρώσκεται καὶ τὸ αἷμα
ἐς τὸ ὕδωρ ἐρχόμενον ἀλλάσσει τὸν ποταμὸν καὶ τῷ ῥόῳ τὴν
ἐπωνυμίην διδοῖ.   ταῦτα μὲν οἱ πολλοὶ λέγουσιν.   ἐμοὶ δὲ
τις ἀνὴρ Βύβλιος ἀληθέα δοκέων λέγειν ἑτέρην ἀπηγέετο τοῦ
πάθεος αἰτίην.   ἔλεγε δὲ ὧδε· ὁ Ἄδωνις ὁ ποταμός, ὦ
ξεῖνε, διὰ τοῦ Λιβάνου ἔρχεται· ὁ δὲ Λίβανος κάρτα
ξανθόγεώς ἐστιν· ἄνεμοι ὦν τρηχέες ἐκείνῃσι τῇσιν ἡμέρῃσιν
ἱστάμενοι τὴν γῆν τῷ ποταμῷ ἐπιφέρουσι ἐοῦσαν ἐς τὰ μάλιστα μιλτώδεα, ἡ δὲ γῆ μιν αἱμώδεα τίθησι· καὶ τοῦδε τοῦ
πάθεος οὐ τὸ αἷμα, τὸ λέγουσιν, ἀλλ' ἡ χώρη αἰτίη.   ὁ μέν
μοι Βύβλιος

---

1. καὶ τοῦτο - τὸ καὶ N: added to ΓΕ by a later
hand.

penalty: For a single day they stand offering their
beauty for sale. The market, however, is open to
foreigners only and the payment becomes an offering
to Aphrodite.

7   There are some inhabitants of Byblos who say that
the Egyptian Osiris is buried among them and that all
the laments and the rites are performed not for Adonis
but for Osiris. I will also tell you on what grounds
they consider this account to be reliable. Each year
a head comes from Egypt to Byblos, making the voyage
in seven days, and the winds carry it by divine guid-
ance. It does not turn aside in any direction, but
comes only to Byblos. This is quite miraculous. It
occurs every year; indeed, it happened while I was
present in Byblos and I saw the "Byblian" head.[1]

8   There is also another marvel in the land of Byblos. A river from Mount Lebanon empties into the sea.
Adonis is the name given to the river. Each year the
river becomes blood red and, having changed its color,
flows into the sea and reddens a large part of it,
giving a signal for lamentations to the inhabitants
of Byblos. They tell the story that on these days
Adonis is being wounded up on Mt. Lebanon and his
blood, as it goes into the water, alters the river and
gives the stream its name. This is the general version, but a certain man of Byblos, who seemed to me to
be telling the truth, recounted another reason for the
phenomenon. This is his account: "The River Adonis,
stranger, comes through the Lebanon and Mt. Lebanon
has a quite ruddy soil. Then strong winds come up on
these days and deposit the earth, which is quite red,
in the river, and the soil makes it blood red. The
cause of this phenomenon is not the blood, as people
say, but it is the land." This is the account which

---

1. There may be an untranslatable pun in these words:
They can mean "the head that came from Byblos," or "the
head made of papyrus."

τοσαῦτα ἀπηγέετο· εἰ δὲ ἀτρεκέως ταῦτα ἔλεγεν, ἐμοὶ μὲν
δοκέει κάρτα θείη καὶ τοῦ ἀνέμου ἡ συντυχίη. 9. ἀνέβην δὲ
καὶ ἐς τὸν Λίβανον, ἐκ Βύβλου ὁδὸν ἡμέρης, πυθόμενος
αὐτόθι ἀρχαῖον ἱρὸν 'Αφροδίτης ἔμμεναι, τὸ Κινύρης εἴσατο,
καὶ εἶδον τὸ ἱρὸν καὶ ἀρχαῖον ἦν. τάδε μέν ἐστι τὰ ἐν τῇ
Συρίη ἀρχαῖα καὶ μεγάλα ἱρά. 10. τοσούτων δὲ ἐόντων ἐμοὶ
δοκέει οὐδὲν τῶν ἐν τῇ ἱρῇ πόλι μεῖζον ἔμμεναι οὐδὲ νηὸς
ἄλλος ἁγιώτερος οὐδὲ χώρη ἄλλη ἱροτέρη. ἔνι δὲ καὶ ἔργα
ἐν αὐτῷ πολυτελέα καὶ ἀρχαῖα ἀναθήματα καὶ πολλὰ θωύματα
καὶ ξόανα θεοπρεπέα, καὶ θεοὶ δὲ κάρτα αὐτοῖσιν ἐμφανέες·
ἱδρώει γὰρ δὴ ὦν παρὰ σφίσι τὰ ξόανα καὶ κινέεται καὶ
χρησμηγορέει· καὶ βοὴ δὲ πολλάκις ἐγένετο ἐν τῷ νηῷ
κλεισθέντος τοῦ ἱροῦ, καὶ πολλοὶ ἤκουσαν. ναὶ μὴν καὶ
ὄλβου πέρι ἐν τοῖσιν ἐγὼ οἶδα πρῶτόν ἐστι· πολλὰ γὰρ
αὐτοῖσιν ἀπικνέεται χρήματα ἔκ τε 'Αραβίης καὶ Φοινίκων
καὶ Βαβυλωνίων καὶ ἄλλα ἐκ Καππαδοκίης, τὰ δὲ καὶ Κίλικες
φέρουσι, τὰ δὲ 'Ασσύριοι. εἶδον δὲ ἐγὼ καὶ τὰ ἐν τῷ νηῷ
λάθρη ἀποκέαται, ἐσθῆτα πολλὴν καὶ ἄλλα ὁκόσα ἐς ἄργυρον
ἢ ἐς χρυσὸν ἀποκέκριται· ὁρταὶ μὲν γὰρ καὶ πανηγύριες
οὐδαμοῖσιν ἄλλοισιν ἀνθρώπων τοσαίδε ἀποδεδέχαται.
11. ἱστορέοντι δέ μοι ἐτέων πέρι, ὁκόσα τῷ ἱρῷ ἐστι, καὶ
τὴν θεὸν αὐτοὶ ἥντινα δοκέουσι, πολλοὶ λόγοι ἐλέγοντο, τῶν
οἱ μὲν ἱροί, οἱ δὲ ἐμφανέες, οἱ δὲ κάρτα μυθώδεες, καὶ
ἄλλοι βάρβαροι, οἱ μὲν τοῖσιν Ἕλλησιν ὁμολογέοντες, τοὺς
ἐγὼ πάντας μὲν ἐρέω, δέκομαι δὲ οὐδαμά.

the man of Byblos gave me, but even if his version is
correct, I consider the chance intervention of the
wind quite divine.

9   Then I went up onto the Lebanon, a day's journey
from Byblos, upon learning that an ancient sanctuary
of Aphrodite, which Cinyras founded, was there. I saw
the sanctuary, and it is an ancient one. These then
are the ancient and great sanctuaries in Syria.

10   But even if they are like this, it seems to me
that none of them is greater than those in the Holy
City, nor could any other temple be more sacred nor
any other region more holy. In the temple are many
expensive artifacts and ancient offerings, many marvelous things and statues befitting the gods. More-
over, gods are readily manifest to the inhabitants.
For the statues among them sweat and move about and
give oracles, and a shouting often occurs in the temple when the sanctuary is locked, and many have heard
it. Certainly in regards to wealth it is foremost
among the places which I know about. For many trea-
sures come to them from Arabia, Phoenicia and Babylon-
ia and still more from Cappadocia. The Assyrians as
well as the Cilicians bring some. --I saw also what
is secretly stored in the temple, much clothing and
other items separated into silver or gold. --For in
the matter of feasts and festivals, among no other
peoples have so many been designated.

11   When I enquired about the age of the temple and
whom they consider its goddess to be, I heard many
accounts. Some of them were sacred, some profane,
some quite fabulous. Some were barbarian, and some
agree with what the Greeks tell. I will tell them
all, but in no way do I accept them.

18

12. οἱ μὲν ὦν πολλοὶ Δευκαλίωνα τὸν Σισύθεα¹ τὸ ἱρὸν
εἴσασθαι λέγουσι, τοῦτον Δευκαλίωνα, ἐπὶ τοῦ τὸ πολλὸν
ὕδωρ ἐγένετο. Δευκαλίωνος δὲ πέρι λόγον ἐν Ἕλλησιν
ἤκουσα, τὸν Ἕλληνες ἐπ' αὐτῷ λέγουσιν. ὁ δὲ μῦθος ὧδε
ἔχει· ἥδε ἡ γενεὴ οἱ νῦν ἄνθρωποι οὐ πρῶτοι ἐγένοντο,
ἀλλ' ἐκείνη μὲν ἡ γενεὴ πάντες ὤλοντο. οὗτοι δὲ γένεος
τοῦ δευτέρου εἰσί, τὸ αὖτις ἐκ Δευκαλίωνος ἐς πληθὺν
ἀπίκετο. ἐκείνων δὲ πέρι τῶν ἀνθρώπων τάδε μυθέονται·
ὑβρισταὶ κάρτα ἐόντες ἀθέμιστα ἔργα ἔπρησσον, οὔτε γὰρ
ὅρκια ἐφύλασσον οὔτε ξείνους ἐδέκοντο οὔτε ἱκετέων
ἠνείχοντο, ἀντ' ὦν σφίσιν ἡ μεγάλη συμφορὴ ἀπίκετο.
αὐτίκα ἡ γῆ πολλὸν ὕδωρ ἐκδιδοῖ καὶ ὄμβροι μεγάλοι ἐγένοντο καὶ οἱ ποταμοὶ κατέβησαν μέζονες καὶ ἡ θάλασσα ἐπὶ
πολλὸν ἀνέβη, ἐς ὃ πάντα ὕδωρ ἐγένοντο καὶ πάντες ὤλοντο,
Δευκαλίων δὲ μοῦνος ἀνθρώπων ἐλίπετο ἐς γενεὴν δευτέρην
εὐβουλίης τε καὶ τοῦ εὐσεβέος εἵνεκα. ἡ δέ οἱ σωτηρίη
ἥδε ἐγένετο· λάρνακα μεγάλην, τὴν αὐτὸς εἶχεν, ἐς ταύτην
ἐσβιβάσας παῖδάς τε καὶ γυναῖκας ἑωυτοῦ ἐσέβη· ἐσβαίνοντι
δέ οἱ ἀπίκοντο σύες καὶ ἵπποι καὶ λεόντων γένεα καὶ ὄφιες
καὶ ἄλλα ὁκόσα ἐν γῇ νέμονται, πάντα ἐς ζεύγεα. ὁ δὲ
πάντα ἐδέκετο, καί μιν οὐκ ἐσίνοντο, ἀλλὰ σφίσι μεγάλη
διόθεν φιλίη ἐγένετο. καὶ ἐν μιῇ λάρνακι πάντες ἔπλευσαν,

---

1. Σισύθεα Buttmann, Dind. Jac.: Σκύθεα MSS, Harm.

12   Well then, the majority say that Deucalion,
called Sisythes,[1] founded the sanctuary. This is the
Deucalion in whose lifetime the flood occurred. About
Deucalion I have heard an account among the Greeks,
which the Greeks tell about him.[2] The story goes as
follows:

This race, the men of the present time, was not
the first. As for that previous race, all in it perished. These current men are of the second race,
which multiplied again from Deucalion. Concerning
those earlier men they say the following. They were
extremely violent and committed lawless deeds, for
they neither kept oaths nor welcomed strangers nor
spared suppliants. As punishment for these offences
the great disaster came upon them. Suddenly the
earth poured forth a flood of water. Heavy rains
fell, rivers rushed down in torrents, and the sea rose
on high, until everything became water,[3] and all the
people perished. Deucalion alone among men was left
for the second race because of his prudence and piety.
This was the manner of his salvation: He embarked his
children and his wives into a great ark which he pos-
sessed and he himself went in. As he boarded, pigs
and horses, species of lions, snakes and every kind of
creature that grazes on earth came to him, all of them
in pairs. ·He welcomed all, and none harmed him. Instead, from some divine source, there was great
friendship among them, and in a single ark all sailed

---

1. The MSS here read Σκυθέα, i.e. Deucalion, the
Scythian. The emendation is a possible form of Xisouthros,
found in Berossus for Sumerian Ziusudra, the flood hero.
Cf. *Pauly-Wissowa*, *Realencyclopädie* IX.2,2135-38.

2. The Greek style is awkward, in this phrase and
frequently in the following section.

3. For πάντα ὕδωρ ἐγένοντο, cf. Ovid, Met. 1:292:
omnia pontus erant. [O'Neil].

ἔστε τὸ ὕδωρ ἐπεκράτεε. τὰ μὲν Δευκαλίωνος πέρι Ἕλληνες
ἱστορέουσι. 13. τὸ δὲ ἀπὸ τούτου λέγεται λόγος ὑπὸ τῶν
ἐν τῇ ἱρῇ πόλι μεγάλως ἄξιος θωυμάσαι, ὅτι ἐν τῇ σφετέρῃ
χώρῃ χάσμα μέγα ἐγένετο καὶ τὸ σύμπαν ὕδωρ κατεδέξατο·
Δευκαλίων δέ, ἐπεὶ τάδε ἐγένετο, βωμούς τε ἔθετο καὶ νηὸν
ἐπὶ τῷ χάσματι Ἥρης ἅγιον ἐστήσατο. ἐγὼ δὲ καὶ τὸ χάσμα
εἶδον, καὶ ἔστιν ὑπὸ τῷ νηῷ κάρτα μικρόν. εἰ μὲν ὦν
πάλαι καὶ μέγα ἐὸν νῦν τοιόνδε ἐγένετο, οὐκ οἶδα· τὸ δὲ
ἐγὼ εἶδον, μικρόν ἐστι. σῆμα δὲ τῆς ἱστορίης τόδε
πρήσσουσι· δὶς ἑκάστου ἔτεος ἐκ θαλάσσης ὕδωρ ἐς τὸν
νηὸν ἀπικνέεται. φέρουσι δὲ οὐκ ἱρέες μοῦνον, ἀλλὰ πᾶσα
Συρίη καὶ Ἀραβίη, καὶ πέρηθεν τοῦ Εὐφρήτεω πολλοὶ
ἄνθρωποι ἐς θάλασσαν ἔρχονται καὶ πάντες ὕδωρ φέρουσι,
τὸ πρῶτα μὲν ἐν τῷ νηῷ ἐκχέουσι, μετὰ δὲ ἐς τὸ χάσμα
κατέρχεται, καὶ δέκεται τὸ χάσμα μικρὸν ἐὸν ὕδατος χρῆμα
πολλόν. τὰ δὲ ποιέοντες Δευκαλίωνα ἐν τῷ ἱρῷ τόνδε
νόμον θέσθαι λέγουσι συμφορῆς τε καὶ εὐεργεσίης μνῆμα
ἔμμεναι. ὁ μὲν ὦν ἀρχαῖος αὐτοῖσι λόγος ἀμφὶ τοῦ ἱροῦ
τοιόσδε ἐστί. 14. ἄλλοι δὲ Σεμίραμιν τὴν Βαβυλωνίην,
τῆς δὴ πολλὰ ἔργα ἐν τῇ Ἀσίῃ ἐστί, ταύτην καὶ τόδε τὸ
ἕδος εἴσασθαι νομίζουσιν, οὔκ Ἥρῃ δὲ εἴσασθαι, ἀλλὰ
μητρὶ ἑωυτῆς, τῆς Δερκετὼ οὔνομα. Δερκετοῦς δὲ εἶδος ἐν
Φοινίκῃ ἐθεησάμην, θέημα ξένον· ἡμισέη μὲν γυνή, τὸ δὲ
ὁκόσον ἐκ μηρῶν ἐς ἄκρους πόδας ἰχθύος οὐρὴ ἀποτείνεται.
ἡ δὲ ἐν τῇ ἱρῇ πόλι πᾶσα γυνή ἐστι. πίστιες δὲ τοῦ λόγου
αὐτοῖσι κάρτα

as long as the flood prevailed. This, then is the
story which Greeks tell about Deucalion.[1]

13   What happened after this, however, is the subject
of a story told by the inhabitants of the Holy City,
and we may rightly be amazed at it. They say that in
their land a great chasm was formed and it took in all
the water. When this happened, Deucalion set up al-
tars and built over the chasm a temple sacred to Hera.
I myself saw the chasm. It is beneath the temple and
quite small. Whether it was large of old, and now
such a size as it is, I do not know. In any case, the
one that I saw is small.

As a symbol of this story they do this: Twice
each year water from the sea is carried to the temple.
Not only priests, but the whole of Syria and Arabia
brings it and from beyond the Euphrates many men come
to the sea and all bring water. First they pour it
out in the temple. Afterwards it goes down into the
chasm, and the chasm, though small, takes in a great
deal of water. In doing these things they claim that
Deucalion established this custom in the sanctuary as
a memorial both of the disaster and of the divine
favor. Such is their traditional account about the
sanctuary.

14   Others, however, think that Semiramis the Baby-
lonian, whose deeds in Asia are many, also founded
this site and that she founded it not for Hera, but
for her own mother, whose name was Derketo. I saw a
likeness of Derketo in Phoenicia, a strange sight! It
is a woman for half its length, but from the thighs to
the tips of the feet a fish's tail stretches out. The
Derketo in the Holy City, however, is entirely a woman, and the grounds for their account are not very

---

1. This is not what our Greek sources relate. Cf.
Frazer's notes to Apollodorus in the Loeb edition, Vol. I,
50-56.

22

ἐμφανέες· ἰχθύας χρῆμα ἰρὸν νομίζουσι καὶ οὔκοτε ἰχθύων
ψαύουσι, καὶ ὄρνιθας τοὺς μὲν ἄλλους σιτέονται, περιστερὴν δὲ μούνην οὐ σιτέονται, ἀλλὰ σφίσιν ἥδε ἰρή. τὰ
δὲ γιγνόμενα δοκέει αὐτοῖσι ποιέεσθαι Δερκετοῦς καὶ
Σεμιράμιος εἴνεκα, τὸ μέν, ὅτι Δερκετὼ μορφὴν ἰχθύος
ἔχει, τὸ δέ, ὅτι τὸ Σεμιράμιος τέλος ἐς περιστερὴν ἀπίκετο. ἀλλ᾿ ἐγὼ τὸν μὲν νηὸν ὅτι Σεμιράμιος ἔργον ἐστί,
τάχα κου δέξομαι· Δερκετοῦς δὲ τὸ ἰρὸν ἔμμεναι οὐδαμὰ
πείθομαι, ἐπεὶ καὶ παρ᾿ Αἰγυπτίων ἐνίοισιν ἰχθύας οὐ
σιτέονται, καὶ τάδε οὐ Δερκετοῖ χαρίζονται. 15. ἔστι
δὲ καὶ ἄλλος λόγος ἰρός, τὸν ἐγὼ σοφοῦ ἀνδρὸς ἤκουσα,
ὅτι ἡ μὲν θεὴ ῾Ρέη ἐστί, τὸ δὲ ἰρὸν ῎Αττεω ποίημα.
῎Αττης δὲ γένος μὲν Λυδὸς ἦν, πρῶτος δὲ τὰ ὄργια τὰ ἐς
῾Ρέην ἐδιδάξατο. καὶ τὰ Φρύγες καὶ Λυδοὶ καὶ Σαμόθρᾳκες
ἐπιτελέουσιν, ῎Αττεω πάντα ἔμαθον· ὡς γάρ μιν ἡ ῾Ρέη
ἔτεμε, βίου μὲν ἀνδρηίου ἀπεπαύσατο, μορφὴν δὲ θηλέην
ἠμείψατο καὶ ἐσθῆτα γυναικηίην ἐνεδύσατο καὶ ἐς πᾶσαν
γῆν φοιτέων ὄργιά τε ἐπετέλεε καὶ τὰ ἔπαθεν ἀπηγέετο καὶ
῾Ρέην ἤειδεν. ἐν τοῖσι καὶ ἐς Συρίην ἀπίκετο. ὡς δὲ
οἱ πέρην Εὐφρήτεω ἄνθρωποι οὔτε αὐτὸν οὔτε ὄργια ἐδέκοντο,
ἐν τῷδε τῷ χώρῳ τὸ ἰρὸν ἐποιήσατο. σημήια δέ· ἡ θεὸς τὰ
πολλὰ ἐς ῾Ρέην ἐπικνέεται.[1] λέοντες γάρ μιν φέρουσι καὶ
τύμπανον ἔχει καὶ ἐπὶ τῇ κεφαλῇ πυργοφορέει, ὁκοίην ῾Ρέην
Λυδοὶ ποιέουσιν. ἔλεγε δὲ καὶ Γάλλων πέρι, οἳ εἰσιν ἐν
τῷ ἰρῷ, ὅτι Γάλλοι ῞Ηρῃ μὲν οὐδαμά, ῾Ρέῃ δὲ τέμνονται
καὶ ῎Αττεα μιμέονται. τὰ δέ μοι εὐπρεπέα μὲν δοκέει
ἔμμεναι, ἀληθέα δὲ οὔ· ἐπεὶ καὶ τῆς τομῆς ἄλλην αἰτίην
ἤκουσα πολλὸν πιστοτέρην.

---

1. ἐπικνέεται Leh., eds.: ἐπικέεται ΓΕ: ἀπικέεται Ν.

clear.[1] They consider fish something sacred and they
never touch one. They eat all other birds, apart from
the dove. For them this is sacred. They think that
these customs came about on account of Derketo and
Semiramis, the first because Derketo has the form of
a fish, and the second because Semiramis ultimately
became a dove. Well, perhaps I accept the temple as
a work of Semiramis, but I certainly cannot believe
that the sanctuary belongs to Derketo. For among the
Egyptians, some people do not eat fish, and they do
not do this to honor Derketo.

15   There is another sacred account, which I heard
from a wise man, that the goddess is Rhea, and the
sanctuary is a creation of Attis. Attis was a Lydian
by birth, and he first taught rites pertaining to
Rhea. All the rites which Phrygians, Lydians and inhabitants of Samothrace perform, they learned from
Attis. When Rhea castrated him, he ceased his male
life-style. He took on instead a feminine form and
donned female clothing. He went out into every land,
performed the rites, related his sufferings and sang
the praises of Rhea. On these journeys he came to
Syria. Since the men beyond the Euphrates accepted
neither him nor the rites, he established the sanctuary in this place. Here is the proof: The goddess is
similar in many ways to Rhea, for lions carry her, she
holds a tympanum and wears a tower on her head, just
as the Lydians depict Rhea. The wise man[1] also said
about the Galli[2] who are in the temple, that Galli
never castrate themselves for Hera, but they do for
Rhea and they also imitate Attis. This explanation
seems plausible to me but untrue, since I heard another reason for the castration which is much more be-
lievable.

---

1. The following is another case of rather simple
and awkward Greek.

2. Galli: the title of certain eunuch priests.

16. ἀνδάνει δέ μοι τὰ λέγουσι τοῦ ἰροῦ πέρι τοῖσιν
Ἕλλησιν τὰ πολλὰ ὁμολογέοντες, τὴν μὲν θεὸν Ἥρην
δοκέοντες, τὸ δ' ἔργον Διονύσου τοῦ Σεμέλης ποίημα· καὶ
γὰρ δὴ Διόνυσος ἐς Συρίην ἀπίκετο κείνην ὁδὸν τὴν ἦλθεν
ἐπ' Αἰθιοπίην. καὶ ἔστι πολλὰ ἐν τῷ ἰρῷ Διονύσου ποιητέω
σήματα, ἐν τοῖσι καὶ ἐσθῆτες βάρβαροι καὶ λίθοι Ἰνδοὶ
καὶ ἐλεφάντων κέρεα, τὰ Διόνυσος ἐξ Αἰθιόπων ἤνεικε, καὶ
φαλλοὶ δὲ ἑστᾶσιν ἐν τοῖσι προπυλαίοισι δύο κάρτα μεγάλοι,
ἐπὶ τῶν ἐπίγραμμα τοιόνδε ἐπιγέγραπται, "τούσδε φαλλοὺς
Διόνυσος Ἥρῃ μητρυιῇ ἀνέθηκα."

'Εμοὶ μέν νυν καὶ τάδε ἀρκέει.[1] ἐρέω δὲ καὶ ἄλλ' ὃ
τι ἐστὶν ἐν τῷ νηῷ Διονύσου ὄργιον. φαλλοὺς Ἕλληνες
Διονύσῳ ἐγείρουσιν, ἐπὶ τῶν καὶ τοιόνδε τι φέρουσιν,
ἄνδρας μικροὺς ἐκ ξύλου πεποιημένους, μεγάλα αἰδοῖα
ἔχοντας· καλέονται δὲ τάδε νευρόσπαστα. ἔστι δὲ καὶ τόδε
ἐν τῷ ἰρῷ, ἐν δεξιῇ τοῦ νηοῦ κάθηται σμικρὸς ἀνὴρ χάλκεος
ἔχων αἰδοῖον μέγα. 17. τοσάδε μὲν ἀμφὶ τῶν οἰκιστέων
τοῦ ἰροῦ μυθολογέουσιν. ἤδη δὲ ἐρέω καὶ τοῦ νηοῦ πέρι
θέσιός τε ὅκως ἐγένετο καὶ ὅστις μιν ἐποιήσατο. λέγουσι
τὸν νηὸν τὸν νῦν ἐόντα μὴ ἔμμεναι τὸν τὴν ἀρχὴν γεγενημένον,[2] ἀλλ' ἐκεῖνον μὲν κατενεχθῆναι χρόνῳ ὕστερον,
τὸν δὲ νῦν ἐόντα Στρατονίκης ἔμμεναι ποίημα, γυναικὸς
τοῦ Ἀσσυρίων βασιλῆος. δοκέει δέ μοι ἡ Στρατονίκη
ἐκείνη ἔμμεναι, τῆς ὁ πρόγονος ἠρήσατο, τὸν ἤλεγξε τοῦ
ἰητροῦ ἐπινοίη· ὡς γάρ μιν ἡ συμφορὴ κατέλαβεν, ἀμη-
χανέων τῷ κακῷ αἰσχρῷ δοκέοντι κατ' ἡσυχίην ἐνόσεεν.
ἔκειτο δὲ ἀλγέων οὐδέν, καί οἱ ἥ τε χροιὴ πάμπαν ἐτρέ-
πετο καὶ τὸ σῶμα δι' ἡμέρης ἐμαραίνετο. ὁ δὲ

---

1. τάδε ἀρκέει MSS: τόδε ἀρκέει Harm.

2. μὴ - γεγενημένον Ald. eds.: ΓΕ lacuna.

16   I like what they say concerning the sanctuary, since they agree in most respects with the Greeks in considering the goddess Hera and the construction a creation of Dionysus, son of Semele. For Dionysus came to Syria on that journey which he made to Ethiopia, and in the temple there are many indications that Dionysus is the founder. Among them are the foreign clothes and the Indian gems and the tusks of elephants, which Dionysus brought from Ethiopia. In addition, two quite large phalli stand at the gateway. On them is an inscription: "These phalli I, Dionysus, dedicated to Hera, my stepmother." As far as I am concerned, this is sufficient proof, but I will tell of another holy object[1] of Dionysus which is in the temple. Greeks erect phalli to Dionysus on which they have something of this sort: small wooden men with large genitals. These are called puppets. This, too, is in the sanctuary. In the right part of the temple sits a small man of bronze with a large penis.

17   These are the tales which they relate about the founders of the sanctuary. Now I shall speak also of the founding of the temple, how it came to be and who built it. They say that the present temple is not the one which was there in the beginning. That was destroyed at a later time, and the present one is the work of Stratonice, the wife of the king of Assyria.

      I think that this Stratonice is the woman whom her stepson loved. A physician's strategem brought his condition to light, for when the misfortune overtook him, he was unable to cope with the ailment, which seemed shameful, and he lay quietly ill. He suffered no pain, but his complexion changed completely and his body grew weaker day by day. When the

---

1. The word ὄργιον here is odd. It usually appears in the plural referring to rites. The fact that it here refers most probably to an object may explain the singular. For examples of the singular, cf. Liddell-Scott-Jones, *Greek-English Lexicon*, s.v. ὄργια, II. 2; Suppl., p. 110, s.v.

ἰητρὸς ὡς εἶδέ μιν ἐς οὐδὲν ἐμφανὲς ἀρρωστέοντα, ἔγνω τὴν
νοῦσον ἔρωτα ἔμμεναι. ἔρωτος δὲ ἀφανέος πολλὰ σημήια,
ὀφθαλμοί τε ἀσθενέες καὶ φωνὴ καὶ χροιὴ καὶ δάκρυα.
μαθὼν δὲ ταῦτα ἐποίεε· χειρὶ μὲν τῇ δεξιῇ ἔχε τοῦ νεηνίσκου τὴν καρδίην, ἐκάλεε δὲ τοὺς ἀνὰ τὴν οἰκίην πάν-
τας· ὁ δὲ τῶν μὲν ἄλλων ἐσιόντων πάντων ἐν ἠρεμίῃ μεγάλῃ
ἦν, ὡς δὲ ἡ μητρυιὴ ἀπίκετο, τήν τε χροιὴν ἠλλάξατο καὶ
ἱδρώειν ἄρξατο καὶ τρόμῳ ἔχετο καὶ ἡ καρδίη ἀνεπάλλετο·
τὰ δὲ γιγνόμενα ἐμφανέα τῷ ἰητρῷ τὸν ἔρωτα ἐποίεε.
18. καί μιν ὧδε ἰήσατο· καλέσας τοῦ νεηνίσκου τὸν πατέρα
κάρτα ὀρρωδέοντα, Ἥδε ἡ νοῦσος, ἔφη, τὴν ὁ παῖς ὅδε
ἀρρωστέει, οὐ νοῦσός ἐστιν, ἀλλὰ ἀδικίη· ὅδε γάρ τοι
ἀλγέει μὲν οὐδέν, ἔρως δέ μιν καὶ φρενοβλαβείη ἔχει.
ἐπιθυμέει δὲ τῶν οὐδαμὰ τεύξεται, φιλέων γυναῖκα ἐμήν,
τὴν ἐγὼ οὔτι μετήσομαι. ὁ μὲν ὧν τοιάδε σοφίῃ ἐψεύδετο.
ὁ δὲ αὐτίκα ἐλίσσετο, Πρός τε σοφίης καὶ ἰητρικῆς μή
μοι παῖδα ὀλέσῃς· οὐ γὰρ ἐθέλων ταύτῃ συμφορῇ ἔσχετο,
ἀλλά οἱ ἡ νοῦσος ἀεκουσίη. τῷ σὺ μηδαμὰ ζηλοτυπέων
πένθος ἐγεῖραι πάσῃ βασιληίῃ μηδὲ ἰητρὸς ἐὼν φθόνον
προξενέειν¹ ἰητρικῇ. ὁ μὲν ὧδε ἀγνὼς ἐὼν ἐδέετο. ὁ δέ
μιν αὖτις ἀμείβετο, Ἀνόσια σπεύδεις γάμον ἐμὸν ἀπαι-
ρεόμενος ἠδὲ ἰητρὸν ἄνδρα βιώμενος. σὺ δὲ κῶς ἂν αὐτὸς
ἔπρηξας, εἴ τοι σὴν γυναῖκα ἐπόθεεν, ἐμεῦ τάδε δεομένου²;
ὁ δὲ πρὸς τάδε ἔλεγεν ὡς οὐδ᾽ αὐτὸς ἄν κοτε γυναικὸς
ἐφείσατο οὐδὲ παιδὶ σωτηρίης ἐφθόνεεν, εἰ καί οἱ μητρυιῆς
ἐπεθύμεεν· οὐ γὰρ ὁμοίην συμφορὴν ἔμμεναι γαμετὴν ἢ
παῖδα ὀλέσαι. ὡς δὲ τάδε ὁ ἰητρὸς ἤκουσε, Τί τοι, ἔφη,
ἐμὲ λίσσεαι; καὶ γάρ τοι σὴν γυναῖκα ποθέει· τὰ δὲ
ἔλεγον ἐγώ, πάντα ἔην ψεύδεα.

---

1. προξενέειν eds.: προξένεις Ν: ΓΕ lacuna.

2. δεομένου cj. Attridge: δεόμενος MSS, eds.

physician saw that he was ill for no apparent reason,
he realized that the ailment was love. There were
many symptoms of concealed love, dulled eyes, voice,
complexion, tears. Once he realized the situation, he
acted as follows: He held his right hand over the
heart of the youth and called everyone in the house-
hold. The youth remained quite peaceful as all the
others came in, but when his stepmother arrived, his
complexion changed, he began to sweat, he was seized
with trembling and his heart pounded. These reactions
made his love obvious to the physician, and he healed
18 him in the following manner. He called the youth's
father, who was exceedingly anxious, and said, "This
ailment from which this lad suffers is not a disease,
but rather guilt. He is suffering no pain. No, love
and frenzy possess him, and he desires things which he
will never obtain, since he loves my wife whom I will
not give up." Now, of course, he told such lies
cleverly.

Then the king immediately begged him, "By your
wisdom and medical skill, do not destroy my son! For
he has against his will suffered this misfortune. His
disease is involuntary. Do not, then, out of spite
bring grief to the whole kingdom and do not, as a physician, introduce murder into your medical practice."
He requested these things in ignorance.

The physician replied immediately, "You insist on
unholy acts, trying to destroy my marriage and using
force on a man of medicine. How would you have acted
if he desired your wife and I made this request of
you?"

The king replied that he would not spare his
wife, nor would he begrudge his son's recovery even
if he desired his stepmother. For losing a wife would
not be a disaster equal to losing a son.

When the physician heard this he said, "Why then
do you beseech me? For he does indeed desire your
wife. Everything I said to you was false."

28

πείθεται μὲν τουτέοισι, καὶ τῷ μὲν παιδὶ λείπει καὶ
γυναῖκα καὶ βασιληίην, αὐτὸς δὲ ἐς τὴν Βαβυλωνίην χώρην
ἀπίκετο καὶ πόλιν ἐπὶ τῷ Εὐφρήτῃ ἐπώνυμον ἑωυτοῦ ἐποιήσατο, ἔνθα οἱ καὶ ἡ τελευτὴ ἐγένετο. ὧδε μὲν ὁ ἰητρὸς
ἔρωτα ἔγνω τε καὶ ἰήσατο. 19. ἥδε δὴ ὧν ἡ Στρατονίκη
ἔτι τῷ προτέρῳ ἀνδρὶ συνοικέουσα ὄναρ τοιόνδε ἐθεήσατο,
ὥς μιν ἡ Ἥρη ἐκέλευεν ἐγεῖραί οἱ τὸν ἐν τῇ ἱρῇ πόλι
νηόν, εἰ δὲ ἀπειθέοι, πολλά οἱ καὶ κακὰ ἀπείλεεν. ἡ
δὲ τὰ μὲν πρῶτα οὐδεμίην ὥρην ἐποιέετο, μετὰ δὲ ὥς μιν
μεγάλη νοῦσος ἔλαβε, τῷ τε ἀνδρὶ τὴν ὄψιν ἀπηγήσατο καὶ
τὴν Ἥρην ἱλάσκετο καὶ στήσειν τὸν νηὸν ὑπεδέξατο. καὶ
αὐτίκα ὑγιέα γενομένην ὁ ἀνὴρ ἐς τὴν ἱρὴν πόλιν ἔπεμπε,
σὺν δέ οἱ καὶ χρήματα καὶ στρατιὴν πολλήν, τοὺς μὲν
οἰκοδομέειν, τοὺς δὲ καὶ τοῦ ἀσφαλέος εἵνεκα· καλέσας δέ
τινα τῶν ἑωυτοῦ φίλων, νεηνίην κάρτα καλόν, τῷ οὔνομα
ἦν Κομβάβος, Ἐγώ τοι, ἔφη, ὦ Κομβάβε, ἐσθλὸν ἐόντα
φιλέω τε μάλιστα φίλων ἐμῶν καὶ πάμπαν ἐπαινέω σοφίης
τε καὶ εὐνοίης τῆς ἐς ἡμέας, τὴν δὴ ἐπεδέξαο· νῦν δέ
μοι χρειὼ μεγάλης πίστιος, τῷ σε θέλω γυναικὶ ἐμῇ
ἑσπόμενον ἔργον τέ μοι ἐπιτελέσαι καὶ ἱρὰ τελέσαι καὶ
στρατιῆς ἐπικρατέειν· σοὶ δὲ ἀπικομένῳ ἐξ ἡμέων τιμὴ
μεγάλη ἔσσεται. πρὸς δὲ τάδε ὁ Κομβάβος αὐτίκα λίσσετο
πολλὰ λιπαρέων μή μιν ἐκπέμπειν μηδὲ πιστεύειν οἱ τὰ
πολλὸν ἑωυτοῦ μέζονα χρήματα καὶ γυναῖκα καὶ ἔργον ἱρόν·
τὰ δὲ ὀρρώδεε μή κοτέ οἱ ζηλοτυπίη χρόνῳ ὑστέρῳ ἐς τὴν
Στρατονίκην γένοιτο, τὴν μοῦνος ἀπάξειν ἔμελλεν.
20. ὡς δὲ οὐδαμὰ ἐπείθετο, ὁ δὲ ἱκεσίης δευτέρης ἅπτεται
δοῦναί οἱ χρόνον ἑπτὰ ἡμερέων, μετὰ δὲ ἀποστεῖλαί μιν
τελέσαντά τι τῶν

The king heeded this advice. He left both his
wife and his kingdom to his son. He himself went off
to the land of Babylon and built on the Euphrates a
city named after himself. There he met his end. Thus
did the physician diagnose and cure love.

19   This Stratonice, while she was still living with
her first husband, had a dream. In it Hera ordered
her to build her a temple in the Holy City and threat-
ened her with many dire consequences if she disobeyed.
Stratonice paid no attention at first, but afterwards,
when a serious illness afflicted her, she described
the vision to her husband, propitiated Hera, and promised to erect the temple. Immediately she became
healthy, and her husband sent her to the Holy City.
Along with her he sent funds and a large escort, some
members of which were to do the building while others
were for security. He summoned one of his friends,
an exceedingly handsome youth by the name of Combabus
and said, "Combabus, among my friends I have special
affection for you, since you are indeed a noble man.
I have nothing but praise for your wisdom and the
goodwill which you have shown us. Now I have a mis-
sion which requires great trust; therefore I want you,
in company with my wife, to accomplish a task for me,
to perform the sacrifices, and to lead the escort.
When you return you will receive great honor from us."

        In response to these words Combabus immediately
made many prayers and begged the king not to send him
nor to entrust to him a sum of money much too great
for him, along with his wife and the holy task. He
dreaded that at some later time he would be the victim
of jealousy because of Stratonice, whom he was going
to escort alone.

20   But when the king was not at all persuaded, Combabus tried a second request. He asked the king to
give him a delay of seven days time and then to send
him out after he had performed a task of utmost

μάλιστα ἐδέετο. τυχὼν δὲ ῥηιδίως ἐς τὸν ἑωυτοῦ οἶκον ἀπικνέεται καὶ πεσὼν χαμᾶξε τοιάδε ὠδύρετο· ὦ δείλαιος, τί μοι
ταύτης τῆς πίστιος; τί δέ μοι ὁδοῦ, τῆς τέλος ἤδη δέρ-
κομαι; νέος μὲν ἐγὼ καὶ γυναικὶ καλῇ ἔψομαι. τὸ δέ μοι
μεγάλη συμφορὴ ἔσσεται, εἰ μὴ ἔγωγε πᾶσαν αἰτίην κακοῦ
ἀποθήσομαι. τῷ με χρῆν μέγα ἔργον ἀποτελέσαι, τό μοι
πάντα φόβον ἰήσεται. τάδε εἰπὼν ἀτελέα ἑωυτὸν ἐποίεε,
καὶ ταμὼν τὰ αἰδοῖα ἐς ἀγγήιον μικρὸν κατέθετο σμύρνῃ
τε ἅμα καὶ μέλιτι καὶ ἄλλοισι θυώμασι καὶ ἔπειτα
σφρηγῖδι τὴν ἐφόρεε σημηνάμενος τὸ τρῶμα ἰῆτο. μετὰ
δὲ ὥς μιν ὁδοιπορέειν ἐδόκεεν, ἀπικόμενος ἐς τὸν βασιλῆα πολλῶν παρεόντων διδοῖ τε ἅμα τὸ ἀγγήιον καὶ λέγει
ὧδε· Ὦ δέσποτα, τόδε μοι μέγα κειμήλιον ἐν τοῖσιν οἰ-
κηίοισιν ἀπεκέετο, τὸ ἐγὼ κάρτα ἐπόθεον· νῦν δὲ ἐπεὶ
μεγάλην ὁδὸν ἔρχομαι, παρὰ σοὶ τόδε θήσομαι. σὺ δέ μοι
ἀσφαλέως ἔχειν· τόδε γάρ μοι χρυσοῦ βέλτερον, τόδε μοι
ψυχῆς ἐμῆς ἀντάξιον. εὖτ' ἂν δὲ ἀπίκωμαι, σῶον αὖτις
ἀποίσομαι. ὁ δὲ δεξάμενος ἑτέρῃ σφρηγῖδι ἐσημαίνετο καὶ
τοῖσι ταμίῃσι φρουρέειν ἐνετείλατο. 21. Κομβάβος μέν
νυν τὸ ἀπὸ τοῦδε ἀσφαλέα ὁδὸν ἤνυεν· ἀπικόμενοι δὲ ἐς
τὴν ἱρὴν πόλιν σπουδῇ τὸν νηὸν οἰκοδόμεον καὶ σφίσι
τρία ἔτεα ἐν τῷ ἔργῳ ἐξεγένετο, ἐν τοῖσιν ἀπέβαινε τάπερ
ὁ Κομβάβος ὀρρώδεεν· ἡ Στρατονίκη γὰρ χρόνον ἐπὶ πολλὸν
συνόντα μιν ποθέειν ἄρχετο, μετὰ δέ οἱ καὶ κάρτα
ἐπεμήνατο. καὶ λέγουσιν οἱ ἐν τῇ ἱρῇ πόλι τὴν Ἥρην
τουτέων αἰτίην ἐθέλουσαν γενέσθαι, Κομβάβον ἐσθλὸν μὲν
ἐόντα λαθεῖν μηδαμά, Στρατονίκην δὲ τίσασθαι, ὅτι οὐ
ῥηιδίως τὸν νηὸν ὑπέσχετο.

importance. He readily obtained this request, went
home, fell on the floor and lamented, "O wretch, why
have I been given this assignment, why have I to go on
this journey, whose result I already see? I am young
and about to escort a beautiful woman. It will be a
great disaster for me unless I remove every cause of
mischief. So I must commit a great deed which will
cure all my fears."

Saying this, he unmanned himself.[1] When he had
cut off his genitals, he put them into a small container with myrrh, honey and other fragrances. Then
he sealed it with a signet which he carried and treat-
ed the wound.

Later, when he felt that he was ready to make the
journey, he came to the king and with many people
present he gave him the container and at the same time
said, "Your majesty, this great treasure, for which I
have special affection, was stored in my house. Now,
since I am going on a long journey, I will entrust
this to you. Keep it safe for me, for it is more pre-
cious than gold, and worth my life to me. When I return, I will take it back in safety."

The king accepted it, sealed it with another signet and ordered his stewards to keep it.

21 So Combabus, after this, made a safe journey.
When they reached the Holy City, they eagerly proceed-
ed to built the temple. They spent three years at the
task, and during this time precisely what Combabus had
feared happened. For Stratonice began to desire the
man who was with her so much of the time, and after a
while she became quite mad for him. Those in the Holy
City say that the cause of it was Hera, who did not
want the noble Combabus to go unnoticed and wanted to
punish Stratonice because she had not readily promised
the temple.

---

1. This expression may be a pun on ἀτελής. Combabus
made himself both incomplete and exempt (i.e. from fear
or evil).

22. ἡ δὲ τὰ μὲν πρῶτα ἐσωφρόνεε καὶ τὴν νοῦσον ἔκρυπτεν,
ὡς δέ οἱ τὸ κακὸν μέζον ἡσυχίης ἐγένετο, ἐς ἐμφανὲς
ἐτρύχετο κλαίεσκέ τε δι᾿ ἡμέρης καὶ Κομβάβον ἀνεκαλέετο
καὶ οἱ πάντα Κομβάβος ἦν. τέλος δὲ ἀμηχανέουσα τῇ
συμφορῇ εὐπρεπέα ἱκεσίην[1] ἐδίζητο. ἄλλῳ μὲν ὦν τὸν
ἔρωτα ὁμολογέειν ἐφυλάσσετο, αὐτὴ δὲ ἐπιχειρέειν αἰδέετο.[2]
ἐπινοέει ὦν τοιάδε, οἴνῳ ἑωυτὴν μεθύσασα ἐς λόγους οἱ
ἐλθεῖν· ἅμα δὲ οἴνῳ ἐσιόντι παρρησίη τε ἐσέρχεται καὶ ἡ
ἀποτυχίη οὐ κάρτα αἰσχρή, ἀλλὰ τῶν πρησσομένων ἕκαστα ἐς
ἀγνοίην ἀναχωρέει. ὡς δέ οἱ ἐδόκεε, καὶ ἐποίεε ταῦτα.
καὶ ἐπεὶ ἐκ δείπνου ἐγένοντο, ἀπικομένη ἐς τὰ οἰκήια, ἐν
τοῖσι Κομβάβος αὐλίζετο, λίσσετό τε καὶ γούνων ἅπτετο
καὶ τὸν ἔρωτα ὡμολόγεεν· ὁ δὲ τόν τε λόγον ἀπηνέως
ἀπεδέκετο καὶ τὸ ἔργον ἀναίνετο καὶ οἱ τὴν μέθην ἐνεκά-
λεεν. ἀπειλούσης δὲ μέγα τι κακὸν ἑωυτὴν ἐργάσασθαι,
δείσας πάντα οἱ λόγον ἔφηνε καὶ πᾶσαν τὴν ἑωυτοῦ πάθην
ἀπηγήσατο καὶ τὸ ἔργον ἐς ἐμφανὲς ἤνεικεν. ἰδοῦσα δὲ ἡ
Στρατονίκη τὰ οὔκοτε ἔλπετο, μανίης μὲν ἐκείνης ἔσχετο.
ἔρωτος δὲ οὐδαμὰ ἐλήθετο, ἀλλὰ πάντα οἱ συνεοῦσα ταύτην
παραμυθίην ἐποιέετο ἔρωτος ἀπρήκτοιο. ἔστιν ὁ ἔρως
οὗτος ἐν τῇ ἱρῇ πόλι καὶ ἔτι νῦν γίγνεται· γυναῖκες
Γάλλων ἐπιθυμέουσιν καὶ γυναιξὶ Γάλλοι ἐπιμαίνονται, ζη-
λοτυπέει δὲ οὐδείς, ἀλλὰ σφίσι τὸ χρῆμα κάρτα ἱρὸν νο-
μίζεται. 23. τὰ δ᾿ ὦν ἐν τῇ ἱρῇ πόλι ἀμφὶ τὴν Στρατονίκην οὐδαμὰ τὸν βασιλῆα λέληθεν, ἀλλὰ πολλοὶ ἀπικνεό-
μενοι κατηγόρεον καὶ τὰ γιγνόμενα ἀπηγέοντο. ἐπὶ τοῖσι
περιαλγέων ἐξ ἀτελέος τοῦ ἔργου Κομβάβον μετεκάλεεν.
ἄλλοι δὲ λέγουσι λόγον οὔτι ἀληθέα, τὴν Στρατονίκην,
ἐπειδὴ ἀπέτυχε τῶν ἐδέετο, αὐτὴν γράψασαν ἐς τὸν ἄνδρα
τοῦ Κομβάβου κατηγορέειν πείρην οἱ ἐπικαλέουσαν, καὶ τὸ
Ἕλληνες Σθενεβοίης πέρι λέγουσι καὶ Φαίδρης τῆς
Κνωσσίης, ταυτὶ καὶ Ἀσσύριοι

---

1. ἱκεσίην MSS: ἀκεσίην Dind.

2. αἰδέετο Leh., Jac., Harm.: ἠδέετο N: ἐδέετο Γ:
ἠδέετο Dind.

22   Stratonice at first was discreet and kept her ailment concealed. When, however, the trouble became too great for her peace of mind, she suffered openly. All day she wept and kept calling for Combabus, and Combabus was everything to her. Finally unable to cope with her misfortune, she sought a decent way to petition him. She was reluctant to confess her love to anyone else, and she was ashamed to make an attempt herself. So she devised this plan: to get drunk on wine and get into conversation with him. For when wine flows in, so does bold speech, and failure is not very shameful, because what happens is forgotten.

      Once she had decided, she acted. When they were coming from dinner, she came to the place where Combabus was lodged. She begged him, grasped his knees and confessed her love. He received her words harshly, denounced her action and accused her of drunkenness. When she threatened to do herself some great harm, he became afraid and told her his whole story. He described all his suffering and he exposed his deed. When Stratonice saw what she never expected, she ceased from her frenzy, but in no way did she forget her love. Instead, she was always in his company as a consolation for unfulfilled love. This sort of love exists in the Holy City even to this day. Women desire the Galli and the Galli go mad for a woman. Yet, no one is jealous, for they consider the matter quite holy.

23   The affairs of Stratonice in the Holy City did not escape the attention of the king. Many who came made accusations and told him what was happening. He was upset by these reports and recalled Combabus from the unfinished task. Others tell a quite erroneous story. They say that Stratonice, when she failed to get what she wanted, herself wrote to her husband and denounced Combabus, accusing him of making an attempt on her. The story which the Greeks tell about Stheneboea and about Phaedra of Knossos the Assyrians also

ἐς Στρατονίκην μυθολογέουσιν. ἐγὼ μέν νυν οὔτε Σθενε-
βοίην πείθομαι οὔτε Φαίδρην τοιάδε ἐπιτελέσαι, εἰ τὸν
῾Ιππόλυτον ἀτρεκέως ἐπόθεε Φαίδρη. ἀλλὰ τὰ μὲν ἐχέτω
ὅκως καὶ ἐγένετο. 24. ὡς δὲ ἡ ἀγγελίη ἐς τὴν ἱρὴν πόλιν
ἀπίκετο ἔγνω τε ὁ Κομβάβος τὴν αἰτίην, θαρσέων τε ἤιεν,
ὅτι οἱ ἡ ἀπολογίη οἴκοι ἐλείπετο, καί μιν ἐλθόντα ὁ βασιλεὺς αὐτίκα μὲν ἔδησέ τε καὶ ἐν φρουρῇ ἔχε. μετὰ δὲ
παρεόντων οἱ τῶν φίλων, οἳ καὶ τότε πεμπομένῳ τῷ Κομβάβῳ παρεγένοντο, παραγαγὼν ἐς μέσον κατηγορέειν ἄρχετο
καί οἱ μοιχηίην τε καὶ ἀκολασίην προὔφερε· κάρτα δὲ
δεινοπαθέων πίστιν τε καὶ φιλίην ἀνεκαλέετο λέγων τρισσὰ
Κομβάβον ἀδικέειν μοιχόν τε ἐόντα καὶ ἐς πίστιν ὑβρίσαντα
καὶ ἐς θεὸν ἀσεβέοντα, τῆς ἐν τῷ ἔργῳ τοιάδε ἔπρηξε·
πολλοὶ δὲ παρεστεῶτες ἤλεγχον, ὅτι ἀναφανδὸν σφέας
ἀλλήλοισι συνεόντας εἶδον. πᾶσι δὲ τέλος ἐδόκεεν αὐτίκα
θνήσκειν Κομβάβον θανάτου ἄξια ἐργασμένον. 25. ὁ δὲ
τέως μὲν ἔστηκε λέγων οὐδέν· ἐπεὶ δὲ ἤδη ἐς τὸν φόνον
ἤγετο, φθέγξατό τε καὶ τὸ κειμήλιον αἴτεε λέγων, ὡς
ἀναιρέει μιν οὐκ ὕβριος οὐδὲ γάμων εἵνεκα, ἀλλ᾽ ἐκείνων
ἐπιθυμέων, τά οἱ ἀπιὼν παρεθήκατο. πρὸς τάδε ὁ βασιλεὺς
καλέσας τὸν ταμίην ἐκέλευεν ἐνεῖκαι τά οἱ φρουρέειν
ἔδωκεν· ὡς δὲ ἤνεικε, λύσας τὴν σφρηγῖδα ὁ Κομβάβος τά
τε ἐνεόντα ἐπέδειξε καὶ ἑωυτὸν ὁκοῖα ἐπεπόνθεεν, ἔλεξέ
τε, ῏Ω βασιλεῦ, τάδε τοι ἐγὼ ὀρρωδέων, εὖτέ με ταύτην
ὁδὸν ἔπεμπες, ἄεκων ἤιον, καὶ ἐπεί με ἀναγκαίη μεγάλη
ἐκ σέο κατέλαβε, τοιάδε ἐπετέλεσα, ἐσθλὰ μὲν ἐς δεσπότεα,
ἐμοὶ δὲ οὐκ εὐτυχέα· τοιόσδε μέντοι ἐὼν ἀνδρὸς ἐπ᾽ ἀδικίην
ἐγκαλέομαι. ὁ δὲ πρὸς τάδε ἀμβώσας[1] περιέβαλέ τέ μιν καὶ
δακρύων ἅμα ἔλεγεν, ῏Ω Κομβάβε, τί

---

1. ἀμβώσας eds: θαμβώσας MSS.

tell about Stratonice. Now, I myself believe that
neither Stheneboea nor Phaedra did such things, especially if Phaedra truly loved Hippolytus. But let
things be as they in fact happened.

24   When the message reached the Holy City, Combabus
knew the cause and went back confident because his defense had been left at home. As soon as he arrived,
the king had him bound and held under guard. Later,
in the presence of the same friends who had also been
there when Combabus was sent forth, he brought him
forward, began to denounce him and charged him with
adultery and licentiousness. With deep emotion he
recalled his trust and friendship, saying that Combabus was guilty on three counts, as an adulterer, as
one who had abused a trust, and as one who acted im-
piously toward the goddess in whose service he had
committed such acts. Many present testified that they
had seen the two of them openly in one another's company. In the end all voted that Combabus should die
immediately, since he had done things deserving of
death.

25   During all this he stood in silence, but as he
was being led off to execution, he spoke up and called
for his treasure, saying that the king was doing away
with him not because of his insolence or because of
any seduction, but because he desired what Combabus
had deposited with him on his departure. In response,
the king summoned his steward and ordered him to bring
what he had given him to guard. When he brought it,
Combabus broke the seal, revealed both what was in the
box and all that he himself had suffered. Then he
said, "Your majesty, I went unwillingly when you sent
me, because I feared this very thing. Since, however,
you forced me, I did something which was noble toward
my master, but unfortunate for me. Nevertheless, even
in this condition, I am accused of a man's crime.

       In response the king cried out, embraced him and
said tearfully, "O Combabus, why did you do this

μέγα κακὸν εἰργάσαο; τί δὲ σεωυτὸν οὕτω ἀεικέλιον ἔργον
μοῦνος ἀνδρῶν[1] ἔπρηξας; τὰ οὐ πάμπαν ἐπαινέω, ὦ σχέτλιε,
ὃς τοιάδε ἔτλης, οἷα μήτε σὲ παθέειν μήτε ἐμὲ ἰδέσθαι
ὤφελεν· οὐ γάρ μοι ταύτης ἀπολογίης ἔδεεν. ἀλλ' ἐπεὶ
δαίμων τοιάδε ἤθελε, πρῶτα μέν σοι τίσις ἐξ ἡμέων ἔσσεται, αὐτέων συκοφαντέων ὁ θάνατος, μετὰ δὲ μεγάλη δωρεὴ
ἀπίξεται χρυσός τε πολλὸς καὶ ἄργυρος ἄπλετος καὶ
ἐσθῆτες Ἀσσύριαι καὶ ἵπποι βασιλήιοι. ἀπίξεαι δὲ παρ'
ἡμέας ἄνευ ἐσαγγελέος οὐδέ τις ἀπέρξει σε ἡμετέρης
ὄψιος, οὐδ' ἢν γυναικὶ ἅμα εὐνάζωμαι. τάδε εἶπέ τε ἅμα
καὶ ἐποίεε· καὶ οἱ μὲν αὐτίκα ἐς φόνον ἤγοντο, τῷ δὲ τὰ
δῶρα ἐδίδοτο καὶ ἡ φιλίη μέζων ἐγεγόνεεν. ἐδόκεε δὲ
οὐδεὶς ἔτι Ἀσσυρίων Κομβάβῳ σοφίην καὶ εὐδαιμονίην
εἴκελος. 26. μετὰ δὲ αἰτησάμενος ἐκτελέσαι τὰ λείποντα
τῷ νηῷ -- ἀτελέα γάρ μιν ἀπολελοίπεεν -- αὖτις ἐπέμπετο,
καὶ τόν τε νηὸν ἐξετέλεσε καὶ τὸ λοιπὸν αὐτοῦ ἔμενεν.
ἔδωκε δέ οἱ βασιλεὺς ἀρετῆς τε καὶ εὐεργεσίης εἵνεκα ἐν
τῷ ἱρῷ ἑστάναι χάλκεον· καὶ ἔτι ἐς τιμὴν ἐν τῷ ἱρῷ
Κομβάβος χάλκεος Ἑρμοκλέους τοῦ Ῥοδίου ποίημα μορφὴν
μὲν ὁκοίη γυνή, ἐσθῆτα δὲ ἀνδρηίην ἔχει. λέγεται δὲ
τῶν φίλων τοὺς μάλιστά οἱ εὐνοέοντας ἐς παραμυθίην τοῦ
πάθεος κοινωνίην ἐλέσθαι τῆς συμφορῆς· ἔτεμον γὰρ
ἑωυτοὺς καὶ δίαιταν τὴν αὐτὴν ἐκείνῳ διαιτέοντο. ἄλλοι
δὲ ἱρολογέουσιν ἐπὶ τῷ πρήγματι λέγοντες ὡς ἡ Ἥρη
φιλέουσα Κομβάβον πολλοῖσι τὴν τομὴν ἐπὶ νόον ἔβαλεν,
ὅκως μὴ μοῦνος ἐπὶ τῇ ἀνανδρηίῃ[2] λυπέοιτο. 27. τὸ δὲ
ἔθος τοῦτο ἐπειδὴ ἅπαξ ἐγένετο, ἔτι νῦν μένει καὶ πολλοὶ
ἑκάστου ἔτεος ἐν τῷ ἱρῷ τάμνονται καὶ θηλύνονται εἴτε
Κομβάβον παραμυθεόμενοι εἴτε καὶ Ἥρῃ χαρίζονται·
τάμνονται δ' ὦν, ἐσθῆτα δὲ οἴδε οὐκέτι

---

1. οὕτω - ἀνδρῶν N: added to ΓΕ by a later hand.

2. ἀνανδρηίῃ Dind., Jac.: ἀνδρηίῃ Harm.

terrible deed? Why did you, of all people, do so un-
seemly a deed to yourself? I do not approve of this
at all. O wretch, to dare what you should not have
suffered and what I should not have seen! I certainly
did not require this defense. Since, however, some
divine power caused this, our first repayment to you
will be the death of the false accusers. Then will
come a great boon, a quantity of gold, silver in
abundance, Assyrian raiment and royal steeds. You
will also have access to us without any to announce
you, nor will anyone bar you from our sight, not even
if I am in bed with my wife." No sooner said than
done. The accusers were led off immediately to execution, while the gifts were given to Combabus and his
friendship with the king became greater. No one of
the Assyrians any longer seemed equal to Combabus in
wisdom or good fortune.

26   Later, when he asked permission to complete the
rest of the temple--for he had left it unfinished--he
was again sent forth. He completed the temple and
remained there for the rest of his life. Because of
his virtue and his service the king allowed him to
erect a bronze statue in the sanctuary. A bronze
Combabus in his honor is still in the temple, a creation of Hermocles of Rhodes. In form it is like a
woman, but it wears a man's clothing.

       The story goes that his dearest friends chose to
share in his misfortune as a consolation for his suffering, for they castrated themselves and followed his
life-style. Others give a religious account of the
matter, saying that Hera, out of love for Combabus,
suggested the idea of castration to many so that he
might not grieve over the loss of manhood alone.

27   This custom, once it began, has remained even to
the present and each year in the sanctuary many castrate themselves and become womanish either as a consolation for Combabus or as an honor to Hera. In any
case, they are castrated. These people no longer wear

ἀνδρηίην ἔχουσιν, ἀλλὰ εἵματά τε γυναικήια φορέουσι καὶ
ἔργα γυναικῶν ἐπιτελέουσιν. ὡς δὲ ἐγὼ ἤκουον, ἀνακέε-
ται καὶ τουτέων ἐς Κομβάβον ἡ αἰτίη· συνενείχθη γάρ οἱ
καὶ τάδε. ξείνη γυνὴ ἐς πανήγυριν ἀπικομένη ἰδοῦσα
καλόν τε ἐόντα καὶ ἐσθῆτα ἔτι ἀνδρηίην ἔχοντα ἔρωτι με-
γάλῳ ἔσχετο, μετὰ δὲ μαθοῦσα ἀτελέα ἐόντα ἑωυτὴν διειρ-
γάσατο. ἐπὶ τοῖσι Κομβάβος ἀθυμέων, ὅτι οἱ ἀτυχέως τὰ
ἐς Ἀφροδίτην ἔχει, ἐσθῆτα γυναικηίην ἐνεδύσατο, ὅκως
μηκέτι ἑτέρη γυνὴ ἴσα ἐξαπατέοιτο. ἥδε αἰτίη Γάλλοισι
στολῆς θηλέης. Κομβάβου μέν μοι τοσάδε εἰρήσθω· Γάλλων δὲ αὖτις ἐγὼ λόγῳ ὑστέρῳ μεμνήσομαι τομῆς τε αὐτέων,
ὅκως τάμνονται, καὶ ταφῆς ὁκοίην θάπτονται, καὶ ὅτευ
εἵνεκα ἐς τὸ ἱρὸν οὐκ ἐσέρχονται· πρότερον δέ μοι θυμὸς
εἰπεῖν θέσιός τε πέρι τοῦ νηοῦ καὶ μεγάθεος, καὶ δῆτα
ἐρέω. 28. ὁ μὲν χῶρος αὐτός, ἐν τῷ τὸ ἱρὸν ἵδρυται,
λόφος ἐστί, κέεται δὲ κατὰ μέσον τῆς πόλιος μάλιστα,
καί οἱ τείχεα δοιὰ περικέαται. τῶν δὲ τειχέων τὸ μὲν
ἀρχαῖον, τὸ δὲ οὐ πολλὸν ἡμέων πρεσβύτερον. τὰ δὲ
προπύλαια τοῦ ἱροῦ ἐς ἄνεμον βορέην ἀποκέκλιται[1] μέγαθος ὅσον τε ἑκατὸν ὀργυιέων· ἐν τούτοισι τοῖσι προπυλαίοισι καὶ οἱ φαλλοὶ ἑστᾶσι, τοὺς Διόνυσος ἐστήσατο,
ἡλικίην καὶ οἵδε τριηκοσίων[2] ὀργυιέων. ἐς τουτέων τὸν
ἕνα φαλλόν[3] ἀνὴρ ἑκάστου ἔτεος δὶς ἀνέρχεται οἰκέει τε
ἐν ἄκρῳ τῷ φαλλῷ χρόνον ἑπτὰ ἡμερέων. αἰτίη δέ οἱ τῆς
ἀνόδου ἥδε λέγεται· οἱ μὲν πολλοὶ νομίζουσιν ὅτι ὑψοῦ
τοῖσι θεοῖσιν ὁμιλέει καὶ ἀγαθὰ πάσῃ Συρίῃ αἰτέει, οἱ
δὲ τῶν εὐχωλέων ἀγχόθεν ἐπαΐουσιν. ἄλλοισι δὲ δοκέει
καὶ τάδε Δευκαλίωνος εἵνεκα ποιέεσθαι ἐκείνης ξυμφορῆς
μνήματα, ὁκότε οἱ ἄνθρωποι ἐς τὰ οὔρεα καὶ ἐς τὰ περι-
μήκεα τῶν δενδρέων ἤεισαν τὸ πολλὸν ὕδωρ ὀρρωδέοντες.
ἐμοὶ μέν νυν καὶ τάδε ἀπίθανα. δοκέω γε μὲν

---

1. ἀποκέκλιται Dind., Jac.: ἀποκέκριται MSS, Harm.

2. τριηκοσίων MSS, Harm: τριήκοντα Dind., Jac.

3. ἕνα φαλλόν N: added to ΓΕ by a later hand.

male clothing. Instead, they don feminine garments
and do the work of women. As I heard it, the reason
for this, too, is attributed to Combabus. For it once
happened to him that a foreign woman came to a festival, saw him, handsome and still wearing male clothing, and fell madly in love. But when she later
learned that he was not a whole man, she slew herself.
As a result of this, Combabus, depressed because he
was unlucky at love, donned female clothing, so that
no other woman would be likewise deceived. This is
the reason for the female garment of the Galli.

This is all I have to say about Combabus. I will
discuss the Galli again in a later section, telling
how they perform their castration, and how they are
buried and why they do not enter the sanctuary. First,
however, my spirit moves me to speak about the situation of the temple and of its size, and I shall so
speak.

28   The site itself, where the sanctuary is built, is
a hill. It lies right in the center of the city and
double walls surround it. One of the walls is ancient,
the other is not much older than we are. The entryway
of the temple faces the north and its height is about
600 feet. In the gateway stand the phalli which Dionysus set up; they are 1800 feet high.[1] A man climbs
up one of these phalli twice each year and lives on
the tip of the phallus for a period of seven days.
This reason is given for the ascent. The populace be-
lieves that he communes with the gods on high and asks
for blessings on all Syria, and the gods hear the
prayers from nearby. Others think that this, too, is
done because of Deucalion, as a memorial of that
disaster when men went to the mountains and the high-
est of the trees out of terror at the flood. Now,
these explanations seem unbelievable to me. I think

1. On this absurdly large number see Harmon's note,
ad loc.

Διονύσῳ σφέας καὶ τάδε ποιέειν, συμβάλλομαι δὲ τουτέοισι·
φαλλοὺς ὅσοι Διονύσῳ ἐγείρουσιν, ἐν τοῖσι φαλλοῖσι καὶ
ἄνδρας ξυλίνους κατίζουσιν, ὅτευ μὲν εἴνεκα ἐγὼ οὐκ
ἐρέω. δοκέει δ' ὦν μοι, καὶ ὅδε ἐς ἐκείνου μίμησιν τοῦ
ξυλίνου ἀνδρὸς ἀνέρχεται. 29. ἡ δέ οἱ ἄνοδος τοιήδε·
σειρῇ μικρῇ[1] ἑωυτόν τε ἅμα καὶ τὸν φαλλὸν περιβάλλει,
μετὰ δὲ ἐπιβαίνει ξύλων προσφυῶν τῷ φαλλῷ ὁκόσον ἐς
χώρην ἄκρου ποδός· ἀνιὼν δὲ ἅμα ἀναβάλλει τὴν σειρὴν
ἀμφοτέρωθεν ὅκωσπερ ἡνιοχέων. εἰ δέ τις τόδε μὲν οὐκ
ὄπωπεν, ὄπωπε δὲ φοινικοβατέοντας ἢ ἐν Ἀραβίῃ ἢ ἐν
Αἰγύπτῳ ἢ ἄλλοθί κου, οἶδε τὸ λέγω. ἐπεὰν δὲ ἐς τέλος
ἵκηται τῆς ὁδοῦ, σειρὴν ἑτέρην ἀφεὶς τὴν αὐτὸς ἔχει
μακρὴν ταύτην, ἀνέλκει τῶν οἱ θυμός, ξύλα καὶ εἵματα
καὶ σκεύεα, ἀπὸ τῶν ἕδρην συνδέων ὁκοίην καλιὴν ἱξά-
νει, μίμνει τε χρόνον τῶν εἶπον ἡμερέων. πολλοὶ δὲ ἀπι-
κνεόμενοι χρυσόν τε καὶ ἄργυρον, οἱ δὲ χαλκόν, τὰ
νομίζουσιν, ἐς ἐχῖνον πρόσθε κείμενον κατιᾶσιν,[2] λέγοντες τὰ οὐνόματα ἕκαστος. παρεστεὼς δὲ ἄλλος ἄνω
ἀγγέλλει, ὁ δὲ δεξάμενος τοὔνομα εὐχωλὴν ἐς ἕκαστον
ποιέεται, ἅμα δὲ εὐχόμενος κροτέει ποίημα χάλκεον, τὸ
ἀείδει μέγα καὶ τρηχὺ κινεόμενον· εὕδει δὲ οὐδαμά· ἢν
γάρ μιν ὕπνος ἕλῃ ποτέ, σκορπίος ἀνιὼν ἀνεγείρει τε καὶ
ἀεικέα ἐργάζεται, καί οἱ ἥδε ἡ ζημίη τοῦ ὕπνου ἐπικέεται. τὰ μὲν ὦν ἐς τὸν σκορπίον μυθέονται, ἱρά τε καὶ
θεοπρεπέα, εἰ δὲ ἀτρεκέα ἐστίν, οὐκ ἔχω ἐρέειν. δοκέει
δέ μοι, μέγα ἐς ἀγρυπνίην συμβάλλεται καὶ τῆς πτώσιος
ἡ ὀρρωδίη. φαλλοβατέων μὲν δὴ πέρι τοσάδε ἀρκέει. ὁ
δὲ νηὸς ὁρέει μὲν ἐς ἥλιον ἀνιόντα.

---

1. μικρῇ Kuster, eds.: μακρῇ MSS.

2. τὰ νομίζουσιν ἐς ἐκεῖνον (ἐχῖνον Harm.) πρόσθε
κείμενον κατιᾶσιν ΓΕ: κομίζουσιν, εἶτ' ἀφέντες ἐκείνου
πρόσθε κείμενα ἀπίασι N, Dind. Jac.

that they do this as well for Dionysus. I make the
conjecture for these reasons: Whoever erects phalli to
Dionysus sets on them wooden men--for what reason I
will not say. At any rate, it seems to me that the
man climbs up in imitation of this wooden man.

29   The ascent is like this: The man ties a short
cord around himself and the phallus; then he goes up
on pieces of wood attached to the phallus, large
enough for his toes. As he ascends, he throws the
cord up on both sides as though he were handling reins.
If someone has not seen this but has seen those who
climb the date palms either in Arabia or in Egypt or
in some other place, then he knows what I mean.

When he reaches the end of his climb, he lets
down another cord which he has. This is a long one,
and with it he hauls up what he wants, wood and
clothes and utensils, from which he puts together a
dwelling like a nest, settles there and remains for
the number of days I mentioned. Many come and deposit
gold and silver, others deposit bronze, which they use
as coin,[1] into a large jar which sits in front and
each person says his name. Someone else stands by and
calls up the name. The climber receives it and makes
a prayer for each person. As he prays, he shakes a
bronze device which sounds loud and sharp when it is
moved. He never sleeps. If sleep ever does overtake
him, a scorpion climbs up, wakes him and treats him
unpleasantly. This is the penalty imposed on him for
sleeping. They tell holy and pious stories about the
scorpion. Whether they are accurate, I am unable to
say. It seems to me that one thing that contributes
greatly to wakefullness is the fear of falling. This
is enough said about the Phallus-Climbers.

---

1. For the text here, cf. A.M. Harmon, "An emendation
in Lucian's *Syrian Goddess*," *Classical Philology* 19 (1924)
72-74.

30. εἶδος δὲ καὶ ἐργασίην ἐστὶν ὁκοίους νηοὺς ἐν Ἰωνίῃ
ποιέουσιν. ἔδρη μεγάλη ἀνέχει ἐκ γῆς¹ μέγαθος ὀργυιέων
δυοῖν, ἐπὶ τῆς ὁ νηὸς ἐπικέεται. ἄνοδος ἐς αὐτὸν λίθου
πεποίηται, οὐ κάρτα μακρή. ἀνελθόντι δὲ θῶυμα μὲν καὶ
ὁ πρόνηος μέγα παρέχεται θύρῃσί τε ἤσκηται χρυσέῃσιν·
ἔνδοθεν δὲ ὁ νηὸς χρυσοῦ τε πολλοῦ ἀπολάμπεται καὶ ἡ
ὀροφὴ πᾶσα χρυσέη. ἀπόζει δὲ αὐτοῦ ὀδμὴ ἀμβροσίη ὁκοίη
λέγεται τῆς χώρης τῆς Ἀραβίης, καί σοι τηλόθεν ἀνιόντι
προσβάλλει πνοιὴν κάρτα ἀγαθήν, καὶ ἢν αὖτις ἀπίῃς,
οὐδαμὰ λείπεται, ἀλλά σευ τά τε εἴματα ἐς πολλὸν ἔχει
τὴν πνοιὴν καὶ σὺ ἐς πάμπαν αὐτῆς μεμνήσεαι. 31. ἔνδοθεν δὲ ὁ νηὸς οὐκ ἁπλόος ἐστίν, ἀλλὰ ἐν αὐτῷ θάλαμος
ἄλλος πεποίηται. ἄνοδος καὶ ἐς τοῦτον ὀλίγη· θύρῃσι
δὲ οὐκ ἤσκηται, ἀλλ' ἐς ἀντίον ἅπας ἀναπέπταται. ἐς
μὲν ὦν τὸν μέγαν νηὸν πάντες ἐσέρχονται, ἐς δὲ τὸν θάλα-
μον οἱ ἱρέες μοῦνον, οὐ μέντοι πάντες οἱ ἱρέες, ἀλλὰ οἳ
μάλιστα ἀγχίθεοί τέ εἰσι καὶ οἷσι πᾶσα ἐς τὸ ἱρὸν μέλε-
ται θεραπηίη. ἐν δὲ τῷδε εἵαται τὰ ἔδεα, ἥ τε Ἥρη καὶ
τὸν αὐτοὶ Δία ἐόντα ἑτέρῳ οὐνόματι κληίζουσιν. ἄμφω
δὲ χρύσεοί τέ εἰσι καὶ ἄμφω ἔζονται· ἀλλὰ τὴν μὲν Ἥρην
λέοντες φέρουσιν, ὁ δὲ ταύροισιν ἐφέζεται. καὶ δῆτα τὸ
μὲν τοῦ Διὸς ἄγαλμα ἐς Δία πάντα ὁρῇ καὶ κεφαλὴν καὶ
εἴματα καὶ ἕδρην, καί μιν οὐδὲ ἐθέλων ἄλλως εἰκάσεις.
32. ἡ δὲ Ἥρη σκοπέοντί σοι πολυειδέα μορφὴν ἐκφανέει·
καὶ τὰ μὲν ξύμπαντα ἀτρεκέϊ λόγῳ Ἥρη ἐστίν· ἔχει δέ τι
καὶ Ἀθηναίης καὶ Ἀφροδίτης καὶ Σεληναίης καὶ Ῥέης καὶ
Ἀρτέμιδος καὶ Νεμέσιος καὶ Μοιρέων. χειρὶ δὲ τῇ μὲν
ἑτέρῃ σκῆπτρον ἔχει, τῇ ἑτέρῃ δὲ ἄτρακτον, καὶ ἐπὶ τῇ
κεφαλῇ ἀκτῖνάς τε φορέει καὶ πύργον καὶ κεστόν, τῷ
μούνην τὴν Οὐρανίην κοσμέουσιν.

---

1. γῆς Longolius, eds.: τῆς MSS.

30   The temple faces the rising sun. In its form and
structure, it is like the temples which they build in
Ionia. A large platform rises above the ground to a
height of 12 feet and on this the temple rests. A
ramp up to it is made out of stone and is not very
long. When one has ascended, the front hall of the
temple presents a marvelous sight, for it is furnished
with doors of gold. From within, the temple gleams
with a great quantity of gold and the roof is all gold.
An ambrosial fragrance comes from it, such as they say
comes from the land of Arabia. And as you approach
even from a distance it sends forth a scent that is
very pleasant. And as you depart, it does not leave
you. Your clothes retain the scent for a long time,
and you remember it forever.

31   In the interior, the temple is not a single unit,
for a second chamber has been made in it. The entry
ramp to it is also short. It is not furnished with
doors, but on the front it is completely open. All
enter the large part of the temple, but into the chamber only priests go, and not even all the priests, but
only those who are particularly close to the gods and
to whom the overall service of the temple is entrusted.
In this chamber are set statues of gods. One is Hera
and the other is Zeus, whom, however, they call by
another name. Both are of gold and both are seated,
but lions support Hera, while the god sits on bulls.

The statue of Zeus certainly looks like Zeus in
every respect: his head, clothes, throne. Nor will
you, even if you want to, liken him to anyone else.

32 As one looks at Hera, however, she presents many different forms. On the whole, she is certainly Hera,
but she also has something of Athena, Aphrodite,
Selene, Rhea, Artemis, Nemesis and the Fates. In one
hand she holds a scepter, in the other a spindle. On
her head she bears rays and a tower and she wears a
girdle with which they adorn only celestial Aphrodite.

ἔκτοσθεν δέ οἱ χρυσός τε ἄλλος περικέεται καὶ λίθοι κάρτα
πολυτελέες, τῶν οἱ μὲν λευκοί, οἱ δὲ ὑδατώδεες, πολλοὶ
δὲ οἰνώδεες, πολλοὶ δὲ πυρώδεες. ἔτι δὲ ὄνυχες οἱ
Σαρδῷοι πολλοὶ καὶ ὑάκινθοι καὶ σμάραγδοι, τὰ φέρουσιν
Αἰγύπτιοι καὶ Ἰνδοὶ καὶ Αἰθίοπες καὶ Μῆδοι καὶ Ἀρμένιοι
καὶ Βαβυλώνιοι. τὸ δὲ δὴ μέζονος λόγου ἄξιον, τοῦτο
ἀπηγήσομαι· λίθον ἐπὶ τῇ κεφαλῇ φορέει, λυχνὶς καλέεται,
οὔνομα δὲ οἱ τοῦ ἔργου ἡ συντυχίη. ἀπὸ τούτου ἐν νυκτὶ
σέλας πολλὸν ἀπολάμπεται, ὑπὸ δέ οἱ καὶ ὁ νηὸς ἅπας οἷον
ὑπὸ λύχνοισι φαείνεται· ἐν ἡμέρῃ δὲ τὸ μὲν φέγγος ἀσθε-
νέει. ἰδέην δὲ ἔχει κάρτα πυρώδεα. καὶ ἄλλο θωυμαστὸν
ἐστιν ἐν τῷ ξοάνῳ· ἢν ἑστεὼς ἀντίος ἐσορέῃς, ἐς σὲ ὁρῇ
καὶ μεταβαίνοντι τὸ βλέμμα ἀκολουθέει, καὶ ἢν ἄλλος
ἑτέρωθεν ἐσορέῃ,[1] ἴσα καὶ ἐς ἐκεῖνον ἐκτελέει. 33. ἐν
μέσῳ δὲ ἀμφοτέρων ἔστηκε ξόανον ἄλλο χρύσεον οὐδαμὰ
τοῖσιν ἄλλοισι ξοάνοισιν ἴκελον. τὸ δὲ μορφὴν μὲν ἰδίην
οὐκ ἔχει, φορέει δὲ τῶν ἄλλων θεῶν εἴδεα. καλέεται δὲ
σημήιον καὶ ὑπ' αὐτῶν Ἀσσυρίων, οὐδέ τι οὔνομα ἴδιον
αὐτῷ ἔθεντο, ἀλλ' οὐδὲ γενέσιος αὐτοῦ καὶ εἴδεος λέγουσι·
καί μιν οἱ μὲν ἐς Διόνυσον, ἄλλοι δὲ ἐς Δευκαλίωνα, οἱ
δὲ ἐς Σεμίραμιν ἄγουσι· καὶ γὰρ δὴ ὧν ἐπὶ τῇ κορυφῇ
αὐτοῦ περιστερὴ χρυσέη ἐφέστηκε. τοὔνεκα δὴ μυθέονται
Σεμιράμιος ἔμμεναι τόδε σημήιον. ἀποδημέει δὲ δὶς
ἑκάστου ἔτεος ἐς θάλασσαν ἐς κομιδὴν τοῦ εἶπον ὕδατος.
34. ἐν αὐτῷ δὲ τῷ νηῷ ἐσιόντων ἐν ἀριστερῇ κέεται πρῶτα
μὲν θρόνος Ἡλίου, αὐτοῦ δὲ ἕδος[2] οὔκ ἔνι· μούνου δὲ
Ἡλίου καὶ Σεληναίης ξόανα οὐ δεικνύουσιν. ὅτευ δὲ
εἴνεκα

---

1. ἐσορέῃ Du Soul, Dind., Jac.: ἱστορέῃ MSS, Harm.

2. ἕδος eds.: εἶδος MSS.

On the surface of the statue is an overlay of gold and very costly gems, some of which are white, some the color of water, many have the hue of wine and many are fiery. There are also many sardonyxes and sapphires and emeralds, which the Egyptians, Indians, Ethiopians, Medes, Armenians and Babylonians bring.

I will tell what is worthy of a longer discussion. Hera bears a stone on her head. It is called a ruby light, and its name conforms with its function.[1] A great light shines from this by night, and the whole temple is illumined by it as if by lamps. By day its glow is weak, although the gem still has a very fiery quality. There is also another wondrous feature in the statue. If you stand opposite and look directly at it, it looks back at you and as you move its glance follows. If someone else looks at it from another side, it does the same things for him.

33   Between the two statues stands another golden image, not at all like the other statues. It does not have its own particular character, but it bears the qualities of the other gods. It is called "Sign" by the Assyrians themselves, and they have not given it any particular name, nor do they speak of its origin or form. Some attribute it to Dionysus, others to Deucalion, still others to Semiramis. Indeed, on its head stands a golden dove. For this reason, then, they say that this "Sign" belongs to Semiramis. Twice each year the statue journeys to the sea to fetch the water which I mentioned previously.[2]

34   In the temple itself, on the left of those entering, there is placed first the throne of Helios, but his image is not on it. For only of Helios and Selene do they not display statues. The reason for this

---

1.   The word for the gem, λυχνίς, is associated with the word for lamp λυχνός.

2.   See section 13.

ὧδε νομίζουσιν, ἐγὼ καὶ τόδε ἔμαθον. λέγουσι τοῖσι μὲν
ἄλλοισι θεοῖσιν ὅσιον ἔμμεναι ξόανα ποιέεσθαι, οὐ γὰρ
σφέων ἐμφανέα πάντεσι τὰ εἴδεα· Ἥλιος δὲ καὶ Σεληναίη
πάμπαν ἐναργέες καὶ σφέας πάντες ὀρέουσι. κοίη ὦν αἰτίη
ξοανουργίης τοῖσιν ἐν τῷ ἠέρι φαινομένοισι; 35. μετὰ δὲ
τὸν θρόνον τοῦτον κέεται ξόανον Ἀπόλλωνος, οὐκ οἷον
ἐώθεε ποιέεσθαι· οἱ μὲν γὰρ ἄλλοι πάντες Ἀπόλλωνα νέον
τε καὶ πρωθήβην ποιέουσι, μοῦνοι δὲ οὗτοι Ἀπόλλωνος
γενειήτεω ξόανον δεικνύουσι, καὶ τάδε ποιέοντες ἑωυτοὺς
μὲν ἐπαινέουσιν, Ἑλλήνων δὲ κατηγορέουσι καὶ ἄλλων,
ὁκόσοι Ἀπόλλωνα παῖδα θέμενοι ἱλάσκονται. αἰτίη δὲ
ἥδε· δοκέει αὐτέοισιν ἀσοφίη μεγάλη ἔμμεναι ἀτελέα
ποιέεσθαι τοῖσι θεοῖσι τὰ εἴδεα· τὸ δὲ νέον ἀτελές
ἔτι νομίζουσιν. ἐν δὲ καὶ ἄλλο τῷ σφετέρῳ Ἀπόλλωνι
καινουργέουσι· μοῦνοι Ἀπόλλωνα εἵμασι κοσμέουσι.
36. ἔργων δὲ αὐτοῦ πέρι πολλὰ μὲν ἔχω εἰπεῖν, ἐρέω δὲ
τὸ μάλιστα θωυμάζειν ἄξιον. πρῶτα δὲ τοῦ μαντηίου
ἐπιμνήσομαι. μαντήια πολλὰ μὲν παρ' Ἕλλησι, πολλὰ δὲ
καὶ παρ' Αἰγυπτίοισι, τὰ δὲ καὶ ἐν τῇ Λιβύῃ, καὶ ἐν τῇ
δὲ Ἀσίῃ πολλά ἐστιν. ἀλλὰ τὰ μὲν οὔτε ἱρέων ἄνευ οὔτε
προφητέων φθέγγονται, ὅδε δὲ αὐτός τε κινέεται καὶ τὴν
μαντηίην ἐς τέλος αὐτουργέει. τρόπος δὲ αὐτῆς τοιόσδε·
εὖτ' ἂν ἐθέλῃ χρησμηγορέειν, ἐν τῇ ἕδρῃ πρῶτα κινέεται·
οἱ δέ μιν ἱρέες αὐτίκα ἀείρουσιν. ἢν δὲ μὴ ἀείρωσι, ὁ
δὲ ἱδρώει καὶ ἐς μέζον ἔτι κινέεται. εὖτ' ἂν δὲ
ὑποδύντες φέρωσιν, ἄγει σφέας πάντη περιδινέων καὶ ἐς
ἄλλον ἐξ ἑτέρου μεταπηδέων. τέλος ὁ ἀρχιρεὺς ἀντιάσας
ἐπερέεται μιν περὶ ἁπάντων πρηγμάτων· ὁ δὲ ἢν τι μὴ
ἐθέλῃ ποιέεσθαι, ὀπίσω ἀναχωρέει, ἢν δέ τι ἐπαινέῃ,
ἄγει ἐς τὸ πρόσω τοὺς προφέροντας ὅκωσπερ ἡνιοχέων.
οὕτως μὲν συναγείρουσι τὰ θέσφατα καὶ οὔτε

custom I also discovered. They say it is right to
make images for the other gods, for their forms are
not visible to everyone, but Helios and Selene are
completely visible and all see them. So, what reason
is there to make statues of those gods who appear in
the open air?

35   Behind this throne stands a statue of Apollo, but
not as it is usually made. For all others think of
Apollo as young and show him in the prime of youth.
Only these people display a statue of a bearded Apollo.
In acting in this way they commend themselves and ac-
cuse the Greeks and anyone else who worships Apollo as
a youth. They reason like this. They think it utter
stupidity to make the forms of the gods imperfect, and
they consider youth an imperfect state. They make yet
another innovation in their Apollo, for they alone
adorn Apollo with clothing.

36   About his deeds I could say a great deal, but I
will describe only what is especially remarkable.
I will first mention the oracle. There are many
oracles among the Greeks, many among the Egyptians,
some in Libia and many in Asia. None of the others,
however, speaks without priests or prophets. This
god takes the initiative himself and completes
the oracle of his own accord. This is his method.
Whenever he wishes to deliver an oracle, he first
moves on his throne, and the priests immediately lift
him up. If they do not lift him, he begins to sweat
and moves still more. When they put him on their
shoulders and carry him, he leads them in every direction as he spins around and leaps from one place to
another. Finally the chief priest meets him face to
face and asks him about all sorts of things. If the
god does not want something done, he moves backwards.
If he approves of something, like a charioteer he
leads forward those who are carrying him. In this
manner they collect the divine utterances, and without

ἱρὸν πρῆγμα οὐδὲν οὔτε ἴδιον τούτου ἄνευ ποιέουσι. λέγει
δὲ καὶ τοῦ ἔτεος πέρι καὶ τῶν ὡρέων αὐτοῦ πασέων, καὶ
ὁκότε οὐκ ἔρονται.[1] λέγει δὲ καὶ τοῦ σημηίου πέρι, κότε
χρή μιν ἀποδημέειν τὴν εἶπον ἀποδημίην. 37. ἐρέω δὲ
καὶ ἄλλο, τὸ ἐμεῦ παρεόντος ἔπρηξεν. οἱ μέν μιν ἱρέες
ἀείροντες ἔφερον, ὁ δὲ τοὺς μὲν ἐν γῇ κάτω ἔλιπεν, αὐτὸς
δὲ ἐν τῷ ἠέρι μοῦνος ἐφορέετο. 38. μετὰ δὲ τὸν Ἀπόλλωνα ξόανόν ἐστιν Ἄτλαντος, μετὰ δὲ Ἑρμέω καὶ Εἰ-
λειθυίης.

39. Τὰ μὲν ὦν ἐντὸς τοῦ νηοῦ ὧδε κεκοσμέαται· ἔξω
δὲ βωμός τις κέεται μέγας χάλκεος. ἐν δὲ καὶ ἄλλα ξόανα
μυρία χάλκεα βασιλέων τε καὶ ἱρέων· καταλέξω δὲ τῶν
μάλιστα ἄξιον μνήσασθαι. ἐν ἀριστερῇ τοῦ νεὼ Σεμιράμιος
ξόανον ἕστηκεν ἐν δεξιῇ τὸν νηὸν ἐπιδεικνύουσα. ἀνέστη
δὲ δι' αἰτίην τοιήνδε· ἀνθρώποισιν, ὁκόσοι Συρίην
οἰκέουσι, νόμον ἐποιέετο ἑωυτὴν μὲν ὅκως θεὸν ἱλάσκεσθαι,
θεῶν δὲ τῶν ἄλλων καὶ αὐτῆς Ἥρης ἀλογέειν. καὶ ὧδε
ἐποίεον. μετὰ δὲ ὥς οἱ θεόθεν ἀπίκοντο νοῦσοί τε καὶ
συμφοραὶ[2] καὶ ἄλγεα, μανίης μὲν ἐκείνης ἀπεπαύσατο καὶ
θνητὴν ἑωυτὴν ὡμολόγεε καὶ τοῖσιν ὑπηκόοισιν αὖτις ἐκέλευεν ἐς Ἥρην τρέπεσθαι. τούνεκα δὴ ἔτι τοιήδε ἀνέστηκε
τοῖσιν ἀπικνεομένοισι τὴν Ἥρην ἱλάσκεσθαι δεικνύουσα
καὶ θεὸν οὐκέτι ἑωυτήν, ἀλλ' ἐκείνην ὁμολογέουσα.
40. εἶδον δὲ καὶ αὐτόθι Ἑλένης ἄγαλμα καὶ Ἑκάβης καὶ
Ἀνδρομάχης καὶ Πάριδος καὶ Ἕκτορος καὶ Ἀχιλλέως.
εἶδον δὲ καὶ Νιρέως ἕδος[3] τοῦ Ἀγλαΐης καὶ Φιλομήλην
καὶ Πρόκνην ἔτι γυναῖκας, καὶ αὐτὸν Τηρέα ὄρνιθα, καὶ
ἄλλο ἄγαλμα Σεμιράμιος καὶ Κομβάβου τὸ κατέλεξα, καὶ
Στρατονίκης κάρτα καλὸν καὶ Ἀλεξάνδρου

1. ἔρονται Frit., eds.: ἔσονται MSS.

2. συμφοραί N, Du Soul, eds.: συμφορή ΓΕ.

3. ἕδος Dind., Jac.: εἶδος MSS, Harm.

this ritual they conduct no religious or personal
business. The god also speaks of the year and of all
its seasons, even when they do not ask. He also talks
about the "Sign," when it must make the journey which
37 I have mentioned.[1] I will tell something else which
he did while I was present. The priests were lifting
him up and beginning to carry him, but he left them
below on the ground and went off alone into the air.
38 Behind the statue of Apollo is one of Atlas, and behind that is one of Hermes and one of Eileithyia.

39   The objects within the temple are arrayed in the
way we have described. Outside stands a large bronze
altar. Also there are myriads of other bronze statues
of kings and priests. I will enumerate the especially
memorable ones. On the left of the temple stands a
statue of Semiramis indicating the temple on her right.
She was set up for this reason: She established a law
for the inhabitants of Syria that they should worship
her as a goddess and that they should ignore the other
deities, even Hera herself, and this they did. Later,
when the diseases, disasters and sorrows sent by the
gods came upon them, she ceased from her madness, ad-
mitted her mortality, and ordered her subjects to turn
once again to Hera. Therefore she still stands like
this, demonstrating to those who come that they should
worship Hera, and confessing that she is no longer a
goddess but that the other is.

40   I also saw there statues of Helen, Hecabe, Andro-
mache, Paris, Hector and Achilles. I also saw an image of Nereus, son of Aglaie, and of Philomele and
Procne, when they were still women, and of Tereus himself as a bird and another statue of Semiramis and the
one of Combabus which I have described,[2] and a very
beautiful image of Stratonice, and one of Alexander

1. See section 33.

2. See section 26.

αὐτῷ ἐκείνῳ ἴκελον. παρὰ δέ οἱ Σαρδανάπαλλος ἕστηκεν
ἄλλῃ μορφῇ καὶ ἄλλῃ στολῇ. 41. ἐν δὲ τῇ αὐλῇ ἄφετοι
νέμονται βόες μεγάλοι καὶ ἵπποι καὶ αἰετοὶ καὶ ἄρκτοι
καὶ λέοντες, καὶ ἀνθρώπους οὐδαμὰ σίνονται, ἀλλὰ πάντες
ἱροί τέ εἰσι καὶ χειροήθεες. 42. ἱρέες δὲ αὐτοῖσι
πολλοὶ ἀποδεδέχαται, τῶν οἱ μὲν τὰ ἱρήια σφάζουσιν, οἱ
δὲ σπονδηφορέουσιν, ἄλλοι δὲ πυρφόροι καλέονται καὶ
ἄλλοι παραβώμιοι· ἐπ' ἐμεῦ δὲ πλείονες καὶ τριηκοσίων
ἐς τὴν θυσίην ἀπικνέοντο. ἐσθὴς δὲ αὐτέοισι πᾶσα λευκή,
καὶ πῖλον ἐπὶ τῇ κεφαλῇ ἔχουσιν. ἀρχιρεὺς δὲ ἄλλος
ἑκάστου ἔτεος ἐπιγίγνεται, πορφυρέην τε μοῦνος οὗτος
φορέει καὶ τιάρῃ χρυσέῃ ἀναδέεται. 43. ἔστι δὲ καὶ
ἄλλο πλῆθος ἀνθρώπων ἱρῶν αὐλητέων τε καὶ συριστέων καὶ
Γάλλων, καὶ γυναῖκες ἐπιμανέες τε καὶ φρενοβλαβέες.
44. θυσίη δὲ δὶς ἑκάστης ἡμέρης ἐπιτελέεται, ἐς τὴν
πάντες ἀπικνέονται. Διὶ μὲν ὦν κατ' ἡσυχίην θύουσιν
οὔτε ἀείδοντες οὔτε αὐλέοντες. εὖτ' ἂν δὲ τῇ Ἥρῃ
κατάρχωνται, ἀείδουσί τε καὶ αὐλέουσι καὶ κρόταλα ἐπι-
κροτέουσι. καί μοι τούτου πέρι σαφὲς οὐδὲν εἰπεῖν
ἐδύναντο. 45. ἔστι δὲ καὶ λίμνη αὐτόθι, οὐ πολλὸν
ἑκὰς τοῦ ἱροῦ, ἐν τῇ ἰχθύες ἱροὶ τρέφονται πολλοὶ καὶ
πολυειδέες. γίγνονται δὲ αὐτέων ἔνιοι κάρτα μεγάλοι·
οὗτοι δὲ καὶ οὐνόματα ἔχουσι καὶ ἔρχονται καλεόμενοι.
ἐπ' ἐμεῦ δέ τις ἔην ἐν αὐτέοισι χρυσοφορέων, ἐν τῇ
πτέρυγι δὲ ποίημα χρύσεον αὐτέῳ ἀνακέετο. καί μιν ἐγὼ
πολλάκις ἐθεησάμην, καὶ εἶχε τὸ ποίημα. 46. βάθος δὲ
τῆς λίμνης πολλόν. ἐγὼ μὲν οὐκ ἐπειρήθην, λέγουσι δ'
ὦν καὶ διηκοσίων ὀργυιέων πλέον ἔμμεναι. κατὰ μέσον
δὲ αὐτῆς βωμὸς λίθου ἀνέστηκε. δοκέοις ἂν ἄφνω ἰδὼν
πλώειν τέ μιν καὶ τῷ ὕδατι ἐποχέεσθαι, καὶ πολλοὶ ὧδε
νομίζουσιν. ἐμοὶ δὲ δοκέει στῦλος ὑφεστεώς[1] μέγας
ἀνέχειν

---

1. ὑφεστεώς Gesener, eds.: ἐφεστεώς MSS.

very much like him. Next to him stood Sardanapallus in an unusual form and with unusual clothing.

41   In the courtyard large bulls, horses, eagles, bears and lions graze at will. They do not harm men at all. Rather all are sacred and tame.

42   Many priests have been appointed for the inhabitants, some of whom slaughter the sacrificial beasts, and some bear the libations. Others are called "Fire-bearers" and others "Altar Attendants." While I was there more than three hundred attended the sacrifice. Their robes are entirely white, and they wear a pilos[1] on the head. A different high priest takes office each year. He alone wears purple and is crowned with

43 a golden tiara. There is also another group of holy men, flute players, pipers and Galli, as well as women, who are frenzied and deranged.

44   Sacrifice is performed twice each day, and everyone comes to it. They sacrifice to Zeus in silence, neither singing nor playing the flute, but when they begin the ceremony to Hera, they sing and play flutes and shake rattles. They were unable to give me a clear explanation about this custom.

45   There is also a lake there, not far from the sanctuary. In it many sacred fish of different kinds are raised. Some of them become quite large. These fish have names and come when they are summoned. When I was there, there was one among them wearing gold. On its fin rests a golden artifact. I often saw the fish, and it always had the object.

46   The depth of the lake is great. I did not test it, but they say that it is more than 1200 feet deep. In its middle stands an altar of stone. At first glance you might think it is adrift and floating on the water and many actually believe that it is, but I think that a great pile stands beneath it and supports

---

1. This was a tall felt cap traditionally worn by eastern priests.

τὸν βωμόν. ἔστεπται δὲ αἰεὶ καὶ θυώματα ἔχει. πολλοὶ
δὲ καὶ ἑκάστης ἡμέρης κατ' εὐχὴν ἐς αὐτὸν νηχόμενοι
στεφανηφορέουσι. 47. γίγνονται δὲ αὐτόθι καὶ πανηγύριές
τε μέγισται, καλέονται δὲ ἐς τὴν λίμνην καταβάσιες, ὅτι
ἐν αὐτῆσιν ἐς τὴν λίμνην τὰ ἱρὰ πάντα κατέρχεται, ἐν
τοῖσιν ἡ Ἥρη πρώτη ἀπικνέεται τῶν ἰχθύων εἵνεκα, μὴ
σφέας ὁ Ζεὺς πρῶτος ἴδηται· ἢν γὰρ τόδε γένηται,
λέγουσιν ὅτι πάντες ἀπόλλυνται. καὶ δῆτα ὁ μὲν ἔρχεται
ὀψόμενος, ἡ δὲ πρόσω ἱσταμένη ἀπέργει τέ μιν καὶ πολλὰ
λιπαρέουσα ἀποπέμπει. 48. μέγισται δὲ αὐτέοισι πανηγύριες, αἳ ἐς θάλασσαν νομίζονται. ἀλλ' ἐγὼ τουτέων
πέρι σαφὲς οὐδὲν ἔχω εἰπεῖν· οὐ γὰρ ἦλθον αὐτὸς οὐδὲ
ἐπειρήθην ταύτης τῆς ὁδοιπορίης. τὰ δὲ ἐλθόντες ποιέουσιν, εἶδον καὶ ἀπηγήσομαι. ἀγγήϊον ἕκαστος ὕδατι σε-
σαγμένον φέρουσι, κηρῷ δὲ τάδε σεσήμανται· καί μιν οὐκ
αὐτοὶ λυσάμενοι χέονται, ἀλλ' ἔστιν ἀλεκτρυὼν ἱρός, οἰκέει δ' ἐπὶ τῇ λίμνῃ, ὃς ἐπεὰν σφέων δέξηται τὰ ἀγγήϊα
τήν τε σφρηγῖδα ὁρῇ, καὶ¹ μισθὸν ἀρνύμενος ἀνά τε λύει
τὸν δεσμὸν καὶ τὸν κηρὸν ἀπαιρέεται, καὶ πολλαὶ μνέες ἐκ
τουτέου τοῦ ἔργου τῷ ἀλεκτρυόνι ἀγείρονται. ἔνθεν δὲ
ἐς τὸν νηὸν αὐτοὶ ἐνείκαντες σπένδουσί τε καὶ θύσαντες
ὀπίσω ἀπονοστέουσιν.

49. Ὁρτέων δὲ πασέων τῶν οἶδα μεγίστην τοῦ εἴαρος
ἀρχομένου ἐπιτελέουσι, καί μιν οἱ μὲν πυρήν, οἱ δὲ λαμ-
πάδα καλέουσι. θυσίην δὲ ἐν αὐτῇ τοιήνδε ποιέουσι·
δένδρεα μεγάλα ἐκκόψαντες ἐν τῇ αὐλῇ ἑστᾶσι, μετὰ δὲ
ἀγινέοντες αἶγάς τε καὶ ὄϊας καὶ ἄλλα κτήνεα ζωὰ ἐκ τῶν
δενδρέων ἀπαρτέουσιν· ἐν δὲ καὶ ὄρνιθες καὶ εἵματα καὶ
χρύσεα καὶ ἀργύρεα ποιήματα. ἐπεὰν δὲ ἐντελέα πάντα
ποιήσωνται,

---

1. καὶ del. Dind. Jac.

the altar. It is always garlanded and has incense, and each day many people, to fulfill a vow, swim out carrying garlands.

47   At that spot great festivals also take place, and they are called "Descents to the Lake," because on these occasions all the sacred objects go down to the lake. Among them Hera goes first, for the sake of the fish, for fear Zeus see them first. For if this happens, they say that all the fish perish. He does come to have a look, but she stands in front of him, holds him off and with many entreaties sends him away.

48   Their greatest festivals are those customarily observed by the sea. About these I have no reliable information to give, for I did not attend the festival myself, nor did I attempt this pilgrimage. I did see what they do when they have returned and I will describe it. Each person brings a vessel filled with water and these are sealed with wax. They themselves do not break the seal and pour out the water. Instead, there is a sacred cock,[1] which lives by the lake. He receives the vessels from them, inspects the seal, and, when he receives a fee, breaks the bond and takes away the wax. Much money is collected by the cock as a result of this activity. Then they carry the water into the temple, pour libations and once they have sacrificed, they return home.

49   Of all the festivals I know about, however, the greatest is the one they hold at the beginning of spring. Some call it "Fire-Festival," others "Lamp Festival." During the festival they sacrifice like this: They chop down large trees and stand them in the courtyard. Then they drive in goats, sheep and other livestock and hang them alive from the trees. In the trees are also birds, clothes, and gold and silver artifacts. When they have made everything ready, they

---

        1. This "cock" might well have been a priest dressed as a bird. Cf. Betz, Lukian, 30f.

54

περιενείκαντες τὰ ἱρὰ περὶ τὰ δένδρεα πῦρ[1] ἐνιᾶσι, τὰ
δὲ αὐτίκα πάντα καίονται. ἐς ταύτην τὴν ὁρτὴν πολλοὶ
ἄνθρωποι ἀπικνέονται ἔκ τε Συρίης καὶ τῶν πέριξ χωρέων
πασέων, φέρουσί τε τὰ ἑωυτῶν ἱρὰ ἕκαστοι καὶ τὰ σημήια
ἕκαστοι ἔχουσιν ἐς τάδε μεμιμημένα. 50. ἐν ῥητῇσι δὲ
ἡμέρῃσι τὸ μὲν πλῆθος ἐς τὸ ἱρὸν ἀγείρονται, Γάλλοι δὲ
πολλοὶ καὶ τοὺς ἔλεξα ἱροὶ ἄνθρωποι τελέουσι τὰ ὄργια,
τάμνονταί τε τοὺς πήχεας καὶ τοῖσι νώτοισι πρὸς ἀλλήλους
τύπτονται. πολλοὶ δὲ σφίσι παρεστεῶτες ἐπαυλέουσι,
πολλοὶ δὲ τύμπανα παταγέουσιν, ἄλλοι δὲ ἀείδουσιν ἔνθεα
καὶ ἱρὰ ᾄσματα. τὸ δὲ ἔργον ἐκτὸς τοῦ νηοῦ τόδε γίγνεται,
οὐδὲ ἐσέρχονται ἐς τὸν νηὸν ὁκόσοι τόδε ποιέουσιν.
51. ἐν ταύτῃσι τῇσιν ἡμέρῃσι καὶ Γάλλοι γίγνονται· ἐπεὰν
γὰρ οἱ ἄλλοι[2] αὐλέωσί τε καὶ ὄργια[3] ποιέωνται, ἐς πολλοὺς
ἤδη ἡ μανίη ἀπικνέεται, καὶ πολλοὶ οἱ ἐς θέην ἀπικόμενοι
μετὰ δὲ τοιάδε ἔπρηξαν. καταλέξω δὲ καὶ τὰ ποιέουσιν· ὁ
νεηνίης, ὅτῳ τάδε ἀποκέαται, ῥίψας τὰ εἵματα μεγάλῃ βοῇ
ἐς μέσον ἔρχεται καὶ ξίφος ἀναιρέεται· τὸ δὲ πολλὰ[4] ἔτεα,
ἐμοὶ δοκέει, διὰ τοῦτο[5] ἕστηκε. λαβὼν δὲ αὐτίκα τάμνει
ἑωυτὸν θέει τε διὰ τῆς πόλιος καὶ τῇσι χερσὶ φέρει τὰ
ἔταμεν. ἐς ὁκοίην δὲ οἰκίην τάδε ἀπορρίψει, ἐκ ταύτης
ἐσθῆτά τε θηλέην καὶ κόσμον τὸν γυναικήιον λαμβάνει.
τάδε μὲν ἐν τῇσι τομῇσι ποιέουσιν. 52. ἀποθανόντες δὲ
Γάλλοι οὐκ ὁμοίην ταφὴν τοῖσιν ἄλλοισι θάπτονται, ἀλλ'
ἐὰν ἀποθάνῃ Γάλλος, οἱ ἑταῖροί μιν ἀείραντες ἐς τὰ
προάστεια φέρουσι, θέμενοι δὲ αὐτὸν καὶ τὸ φέρτρον,

---

1. πῦρ Zucker, O'Neill: πυρὴν MSS, eds.

2. οἱ ἄλλοι MSS, eds.: οἱ Γάλλοι Frit.

3. ὄργια Du Soul, eds.: ὄρκια MSS.

4. τὸ δὲ πολλά Harm: τὰ δὲ πολλά MSS, Dind. Jac.

5. διὰ τοῦτο Dind., Jac.: καὶ τοῦτο Harm.

carry the sacred objects around the trees and throw
fire[1] in, and everything is immediately burnt. Many
men come to this feast from Syria and all the sur-
rounding lands. Each group brings its own holy objects and each has a "Sign" made in imitation of the
one here.

50   On appointed days, the crowd assembles at the
sanctuary while many Galli and the holy men whom I
have mentioned perform the rites. They cut their arms
and beat one another on the back. Many stand about
them playing flutes, while many others beat drums.
Still others sing inspired and sacred songs. This
ceremony takes place outside the temple and none of
those who performs it enters the temple.

51   On these days, too, men become Galli. For while
the rest are playing flutes and performing the rites,
frenzy comes upon many, and many who have come simply
to watch subsequently perform this act. I will describe what they do. The youth for whom these things
lie in store throws off his clothes, rushes to the
center with a great shout and takes up a sword, which,
I believe, has stood there for this purpose for many
years. He grabs it and immediately castrates himself.
Then he rushes through the city holding in his hands
the parts he has cut off. He takes female clothing
and women's adornment from whatever house he throws
these parts into. This is what they do at the Castration.

52   At death Galli do not receive a burial like other
men. Instead, whenever a Gallus dies, his companions
lift him up and carry him to the outskirts of the
city. They set him down along with the bier with

1. Πυρήν as object of ἐνιᾶσιν makes no sense. See
the discussion by F. Zucker, *Orientalia*, n.s. 8 (1939).
383: If one keeps ἐνιᾶσι, one should read πῦρ ἐνιᾶσι (sc.
τοῖσι δένδρεσι); πυρήν may be due to a confusion with the
name of the festival. If, however, one keeps πυρήν,
ἐνιᾶσι must be changed; Zucker proposes to change it to
ἐναύουσι ("they set on fire").

τῷ ἐκόμισαν, ὕπερθε λίθους βάλλουσι, καὶ τάδε πρήξαντες
ὀπίσω ἀπονοστέουσι. φυλάξαντες δὲ ἑπτὰ ἡμερέων ἀριθμὸν
οὕτως ἐς τὸ ἱρὸν ἐσέρχονται· πρὸ δὲ τουτέων ἢν ἐσέλθωσιν,
οὐκ ὅσια ποιέουσι. 53. νόμοισι δὲ ἐς ταῦτα χρέωνται
τουτέοισιν· ἢν μέν τις αὐτέων νέκυν ἴδηται, ἐκείνην τὴν
ἡμέρην ἐς τὸ ἱρὸν οὐκ ἀπικνέεται, τῇ ἑτέρῃ δὲ καθήρας
ἑωυτὸν ἐσέρχεται. αὐτέων δὲ τῶν οἰκηίων τοῦ νέκυος
ἕκαστοι φυλάξαντες ἀριθμὸν ἡμερέων τριήκοντα καὶ τὰς
κεφαλὰς ξυράμενοι ἐσέρχονται, πρὶν δὲ τάδε ποιῆσαι, οὐ
σφίσιν ἐσιέναι ὅσιον. 54. θύουσι δὲ βόας ἄρσενάς τε καὶ
θήλεας καὶ αἶγας καὶ ὄϊας· σύας δὲ μούνας ἐναγέας νομί-
ζοντες οὔτε θύουσιν οὔτε σιτέονται. ἄλλοι δ' οὐ σφέας
ἐναγέας, ἀλλὰ ἱροὺς νομίζουσιν. ὀρνίθων τε αὐτέοισι
περιστερὴ χρῆμα ἱρότατον καὶ οὐδὲ ψαύειν αὐτέων δικαιεῦσι·
καὶ ἢν ἀέκοντες ἅψωνται, ἐναγέες ἐκείνην τὴν ἡμέρην εἰσί.
τοὔνεκα δὴ αὐτέοισι σύννομοί τέ εἰσι καὶ ἐς τὰ οἰκήια
ἐσέρχονται καὶ τὰ πολλὰ ἐν γῇ νέμονται.
55. Λέξω δὲ καὶ τῶν πανηγυριστέων τὰ ἕκαστοι
ποιέουσιν· ἀνὴρ εὖτ' ἂν ἐς τὴν ἱρὴν πόλιν πρῶτον ἀπικ-
νέηται, κεφαλὴν μὲν ὅδε καὶ ὀφρύας ἐξύρατο, μετὰ δὲ
ἱρεύσας ὄϊν τὰ μὲν ἄλλα κρεουργέει τε καὶ εὐωχέεται, τὸ
δὲ νάκος χαμαὶ θέμενος ἐπὶ τούτου ἐς γόνυ ἕζεται, πόδας
δὲ καὶ κεφαλὴν τοῦ κτήνεος ἐπὶ τὴν ἑωυτοῦ κεφαλὴν ἀνα-
λαμβάνει, ἅμα δὲ εὐχόμενος αἰτέει τὴν μὲν παρεοῦσαν
θυσίην δέκεσθαι, μέζω δὲ ἐσαῦτις ὑπισχνέεται. τελέσας
δὲ ταῦτα καὶ τὴν κεφαλὴν αὐτοῦ στέφεται καὶ τῶν ἄλλων,
ὁκόσοι τὴν αὐτὴν ὁδὸν ἀπικνέονται. ἄρας δὲ ἀπὸ τῆς
ἑωυτοῦ ὁδοιπορέει ὕδασί τε ψυχροῖσι χρεόμενος λουτρῶν
τε καὶ πόσιος εἵνεκα καὶ ἐς πάμπαν χαμαικοιτέων· οὐ
γάρ οἱ εὐνῆς ἐπιβῆναι ὅσιον, πρὶν τήν τε ὁδὸν

which they carried him. Then they pile up stones upon
him and after completing this task they return home.
They observe a period of seven days, then enter the
sanctuary. If they enter before this time, they com-

53 mit a sacrilege. In such matters they abide by the
following customs: If anyone of them sees a corpse,
he does not enter the sanctuary that day. On the following day, after purifying himself, he enters. When
the corpse is that of a relative, they observe thirty
days, shave their heads and then enter the temple. It
is sacrilegious for them to enter sooner.

54   They sacrifice bulls and cows as well as goats
and sheep. Swine alone they consider polluted, neither sacrificing nor eating them. Other people consider
them holy, not polluted. Among birds they believe the
dove to be something most holy and they do not think
it right even to touch one. Indeed, if they touch one
inadvertently, they are under a curse for that day.
Consequently, doves are their associates. They come
into their homes and often feed on the floor.

55   Now I will tell what each of the pilgrims does.[1]
Whenever someone is about to come to the Holy City,
he shaves his head and his eyebrows. Then after
sacrificing a sheep, he carves it and dines on the
other parts. The fleece, however, he lays on the
ground and kneels upon it, and the feet and the head
of the animal he puts on his own head. When he prays,
he asks that the present sacrifice be accepted and
promises a larger one for the next time. After fin-
ishing these activities he puts a garland on his own
head and those of everyone making the same pilgrimage.
Then he sets out from his own country and makes the
journey, using cold water both for bathing as well as
drinking, and he always sleeps on the ground, for it
is a sacrilege for him to touch a bed before he

---

1. Cf. section 48.

ἐκτελέσαι καὶ ἐς τὴν ἑωυτοῦ αὖτις ἀπικέσθαι. 56. ἐν δὲ
τῇ ἰρῇ πόλι ἐκδέκεταί μιν ἀνὴρ ξεινοδόκος ἀγνοέοντα·
ῥητοὶ γὰρ δὴ ὦν ἑκάστης πόλιος αὐτόθι ξεινοδόκοι εἰσί,
καὶ τόδε πατρόθεν οἶκοι δέκονται. καλέονται δὲ ὑπὸ
'Ασσυρίων οἵδε διδάσκαλοι, ὅτι σφίσι πάντα ὑπηγέονται.
57. θύουσι δὲ οὐκ ἐν αὐτῷ τῷ ἰρῷ, ἀλλ' ἐπεὰν παραστήσῃ
τῷ βωμῷ τὸ ἰρήιον, ἐπισπείσας, αὖτις ἄγει ζωὸν ἐς τὰ
οἰκήια, ἐλθὼν δὲ κατ' ἑωυτὸν θύει τε καὶ εὔχεται.
58. ἔστι δὲ καὶ ἄλλης θυσίης τρόπος τοιόσδε· στέψαντες
τὰ ἰρήια, ζωὰ ἐκ τῶν προπυλαίων ἀπιᾶσι, τὰ δὲ κατε-
νειχθέντα θνήσκουσι. ἔνιοι δὲ καὶ παῖδας ἑωυτῶν ἐν-
τεῦθεν ἀπιᾶσιν, οὐκ ὁμοίως τοῖς κτήνεσιν, ἀλλ' ἐς πήρην
ἐνθέμενοι χειρὶ κατάγουσιν, ἅμα δὲ αὐτέοισιν ἐπικερτο-
μέοντες λέγουσιν ὅτι οὐ παῖδες, ἀλλὰ βόες εἰσί. 59. στί-
ζονται δὲ πάντες οἱ μὲν ἐς καρπούς, οἱ δὲ ἐς αὐχένας,
καὶ ἀπὸ τοῦδε ἅπαντες 'Ασσύριοι στιγματηφορέουσι.
60. ποιέουσι δὲ καὶ ἄλλο μούνοισιν 'Ελλήνων Τροιζηνίοισιν
ὁμολογέοντες. λέξω δὲ καὶ τὰ κεῖνοι ποιέουσι. Τροιζή-
νιοι τῇσι παρθένοισι καὶ τοῖσιν ἠιθέοισι νόμον ἐποιή-
σαντο μή σφιν[1] ἄλλως γάμον εἶναι, πρὶν 'Ιππολύτῳ κόμας
κείρασθαι· καὶ ὧδε ποιέουσι. τοῦτο καὶ ἐν τῇ ἰρῇ πόλι
γίγνεται. οἱ μὲν νεηνίαι τῶν γενείων ἀπάρχονται, τῇσι
δὲ παρθένοισι[2] πλοκάμους ἱροὺς ἐκ γενετῆς ἀπιᾶσι, τοὺς
ἐπεὰν ἐν τῷ ἰρῷ γένωνται, τάμνουσί τε καὶ ἐς ἄγγεα
καταθέντες οἱ μὲν ἀργύρεα, πολλοὶ δὲ χρύσεα ἐν τῷ νηῷ
προσηλώσαντες ἀπίασιν

---

1. μή σφιν Jac.: μή μιν MSS, Dind., Harm.

2. τῇσι δὲ παρθένοισι Du Soul, Dind., Jac.:
τοῖς δὲ νέοισι MSS Harm.

completes the journey and returns to his own country.

56 In the Holy City a host whom he does not know receives him, for there are specified hosts there for each city and they inherit this family duty. These men are called by the Assyrians "Instructors," because they explain everything to the pilgrims.

57 People do not sacrifice in the sanctuary itself, but when each has brought the sacrificial animal to the altar and has made a libation, he leads it off again alive to his own dwelling. Once there, he sacrifices it and prays by himself.

58 There is another form of sacrifice here. After putting a garland on the sacrificial animals they hurl them down alive from the gateway[1] and the animals die from the fall. Some even throw their children off the place, but not in the same manner as the animals. Instead, having laid them in a pallet, they lower them down by hand. At the same time they mock them and say that they are oxen, not children.

59 All people are marked, some on their wrists and some on their necks. For this reason all Assyrians carry a mark.

60 Another thing they do resembles a custom which occurs among the Greeks only at Troezen. I will tell what these Greeks do. The people of Troezen have a custom for their virgins and young men that they do not marry at all until they cut their locks in honor of Hippolytus, and this they do. This occurs also in the Holy City. The young men make an offering of their beards, while the young women let their "sacred locks" grow from birth and when they finally come to the temple, they cut them. When they have placed them in containers, some of silver and many of gold, they nail them up to the temple, and they depart after each

---

1. Victims may have been thrown from atop the gateway, or, more likely, from the platform at the gateway. Cf. sections 28 and 30.

ἐπιγράψαντες ἕκαστοι τὰ οὐνόματα. τοῦτο καὶ ἐγὼ νέος
ἔτι ὢν ἐπετέλεσα, καὶ ἔτι μευ ἐν τῷ ἱρῷ καὶ ὁ πλόκαμος
καὶ τὸ οὔνομα.

inscribes his name. When I was still a youth I, too, performed this ceremony and even now my locks and name are in the sanctuary.